"Anyone who is about to be married or who is m..
doesn't read *From This Day Forward* is in big troub..
enchantingly wise and wonderful and galvanizing..
which small secrets and large epiphanies are gleaned. From the
time the author orders her new husband to 'Do something with
those potatoes!'—and he begins to juggle them, I was hooked.
I'm so glad I read it and I wish I'd written it."

> —Sherry Suib Cohen
> author of *Secrets of a Very Good Marriage*

"Beautifully written and deeply personal, this is a map to an
often difficult transition. Toni Sciarra Poynter has put her heart
and soul into this journey. These wise words can deepen any
relationship."

> —Gay and Kathlyn Hendricks
> co-authors of *Conscious Loving*

"A sensible, sensitive look at the early years of marriage—
reflecting on the promise, problems, and pleasures. Your love
is sure to grow if you allow yourself to absorb the gentle,
generous, loving attitude that shines through on every page.
A simply beautiful book."

> —Peggy Vaughan
> author of *Making Love Stay*

From This Day Forward

Meditations on the
First Years of Marriage

Toni Sciarra Poynter

**Andrews McMeel
Publishing**

Kansas City

Permissions begin on page 240 and constitute a continuation of the copyright page.

FROM THIS DAY FORWARD: *Meditations on the First Years of Marriage.*
Copyright © 1995, 1998 by Toni Sciarra Poynter. All rights reserved. Printed in the
United States of America. No part of this book may be used or reproduced in any
manner whatsoever without written permission except in the case of reprints
in the context of reviews. For information, write Andrews McMeel Publishing,
an Andrews McMeel Universal company, 4520 Main Street, Kansas City, Missouri 64111.

Book Design by Ralph Fowler
Set in ITC Giovanni Book by TBH*Typecast*

www.andrewsmcmeel.com

A hardcover version of this book was published in 1995 by HarperSanFrancisco.

Library of Congress Cataloging-in-Publication Data
Poynter, Toni Sciarra.
    From this day forward: meditations on the first years of marriage / Toni Sciarra Poynter.
       p.   cm.
    ISBN 0-8362-5326-4 (ppb)
    1. Marriage. 2. Marriage—Meditations. 3. Marriage—Quotations. I. Title.
HQ734.P834   1995
306.81—dc20   94-33041
                                                                                    CIP

For Donald

Acknowledgments

Although this book began in the realm of my own experience—I wrote the book I needed to buy—I certainly never presumed to have the corner on any great truths about marriage. Thanks go to all those whose insights during interviews were cogent, thoughtful, and laced with humor and with their own unique grace, as well as to all those whose casual comments got me thinking and helped me through many times when I feared my well of marital wisdom had run dry.

For the help you gave and for the help you didn't know you were giving, special thanks go to Mackenzie Anderson, Dana Hemmenway, Anthony "A. J." Jackson, Eric Marcus, Fern Martino, "Mo" Matthews, Dona Munker, Sarah Rutta, and Bob Shuman.

To my family and friends, thank you for your enthusiasm and lively interest. You have no idea how much your question, "How's the book going?" actually helped it to "go"!

Many thanks to Barbara Moulton for her sensitive editing and for the good conversation that renews writers.

For my agent, Denise Marcil, thank you for being the first to catch on to my bashful idea, and for your encouragement, confidence, and friendship every step of the way.

Finally, I struggle to find words to thank my husband, Donald, who pushed me out of bed each morning, urging, "Go write epiphanies," who never asked me to change a word of what I wrote about him, and who is my partner for life. Don't worry, sweetheart—I didn't tell anyone that you hang your underwear on the doorknob.

Before You Begin

If you are curious about how to enter this book, I would suggest that you dip into it at will. Get in and out of the entries; find one that suits your mood and see where it takes you. Try a few on and see if they fit; let them incubate in the back of your mind as you go about your daily life.

Of course, you can also start at page one and keep going! This isn't a book that comes with rules about the right and wrong approach. It's a bit like marriage in that regard! The last thing we need in life is a task that feels heavy and arduous. These thoughts are meant to be enjoyed, pondered, smiled at, and shared—maybe with your spouse, maybe with a friend.

Most of all, give yourself time for reflection. Make a space for yourself where you can nurture ideas, insights, and impressions about this journey of marriage. I hope you will receive these meditations in the spirit in which they are offered: as the musings of a fellow traveler.

Purity

"Manifest plainness, / Embrace simplicity, / Reduce selfishness, / Have few desires."
Lao-tzu, *The Way of Lao-tzu*

There are few clearer words than these to describe the highest goods to seek in marriage. When plainness creates truth in word and deed; when simplicity manifests in easy, straightforward communication; when selfishness and desire are set aside so both of you may work for the marriage rather than for the self, there opens up a path we can take to find each other—a fellow striver who is our partner.

Marriage flourishes in the light of pure intentions.

Trinity

Such is the Force of Happiness—
The Least can lift a Ton—
Assisted by its stimulus.
Emily Dickinson, No. 787

Marriage is an entity. It is a "third thing" that is made up of the two of you but that is also greater than the sum of your parts. That's why, when you are really feeling in love and connected, you get a powerful surge of energy, a sense of everything being possible. That is the power of the "third thing" working in you, lifting you out of yourselves, making the two of you greater together than each of you is alone. This transformation is the real miracle of marriage. The two of you have created something that is bigger than you are. Then, having given it life, it becomes *your* life force, infusing you with strength you never had and calling from you a wisdom you never thought to possess. It impels you toward a level of greatness. It demands the best. No wonder it's so heady—and so hard!

In its relentless push toward the apex of our capabilities,
marriage can be the ultimate ecstatic experience.

Take What You Need

"Here are your waters and your watering place. /
Drink and be whole again beyond confusion."
Robert Frost, "Directive"

Your marriage is a place of solace. Return to it often for renewal and sustenance. It will become more and more bountiful the more you take from it. Come home and tell your husband, "I'm so glad to see you. I missed you today." Or, sitting together in the evening, "I need to lean on you." Or, "All I wanted to do all day was to be here, like this, with you." This kind of taking doesn't deplete your marriage; it fills it up with the security of knowing that both of you drink deeply from one well. The more you seek from him, the more he will have and want to give. And the safer he will feel to seek the same from you.

❧

Seek renewal from your marriage.
The more you take, the more will be provided for you.

Being Reborn

"In the beginner's mind there are many possibilities,
but in the expert's mind there are few."
Shunryu Suzuki, *Zen Mind, Beginner's Mind*

When my husband and I announced our engagement, my father said, "Good. Now you can get on with your life." I realized later that Dad had put his finger on precisely the hanging-in-the-balance sensation that both of us had been feeling for months. Our unresolved future, unspoken of, had interfered with necessary life decisions. Was he going to move to the West Coast in search of work and leave me stuck in New York, struggling with a long-distance, uncommitted relationship? Was I going to buy an apartment in an area of town where I knew he didn't want to live? Our lives were on hold until the essential "Is it me or is it we?" question got answered. Deciding to marry placed us on a new track immediately: Our lives no longer ran parallel; they were on one and the same rail.

❧

Marriage begins a life composed of the old yet poised for the new.
It asks you to be again like an infant, wondering and small.

Taking the Plunge

"Oh, must we dream our dreams / and have them, too?"
Elizabeth Bishop, "Questions of Travel"

My mother married when she was eighteen—so young her parents had to give permission for the wedding to take place. The war had accelerated everything: My father was going overseas in three months. Nowadays there are no larger-than-life events to compel two people to leap into the unknown of marriage. There is only the force of our own desire, self-generated and self-accelerated, to push us toward union. No wonder marriage feels like free-fall: We have left a familiar, safe place for the limitless space of the new. No one ever feels truly ready to do that.

Feeling uncertain or fearful about the future does not mean that you are unequal to the journey you have undertaken. It's natural to have doubts when you take on a challenge you have never before attempted. It is natural to fear stepping into the void.

‿◌‿

Those who freely choose their path do so
with deep knowledge of risk.

Be Odd

"All the world is queer save me and thee;
and sometimes I think thee is a little queer."
Attributed to a Quaker, speaking to his wife

B e prepared for people to stand in judgment of the decisions you make in your marriage. Let them say whatever they've got a mind to; raise their eyebrows; sigh and shrug. It doesn't matter. Your marriage has to feel good only to you. It doesn't have to look good to anyone. The sooner you start tuning in to what you need in your marriage rather than to what others need it to be, the sooner your marriage will grow to be a genuine reflection of the vision and dreams of its two creators—you and your husband. And it will fit you like a glove.

All marriages are strange.
Let yours work in its own strange way.

Venture Forth

"All that we do / Is touched with ocean, yet we remain /
On the shore of what we know."
Richard Purdy Wilbur, "For Dudley"

Millions of people do a rare and brave thing: They leap into marriage, a totally unknown terrain. You are one of them. Expect to be confused, fearful, and sometimes lost. If you knew where you were going, you wouldn't be the explorer you are. It's tempting, during our journey, to stay on a well-cut path. But since we are not traveling alone, our path is not only up to us. Our companion may want to try detours or shortcuts. Sometimes he may stop and sit down with his pack, refusing to budge.

When you embark on marriage, a journey is promised. That it will be uneventful is not part of the agreement. Your task is not to make the trip without incident, but to surmount inevitable roadblocks and come out intact on the other side.

❧

*Making a smooth path in marriage is not your responsibility.
The courage to embark and the strength to continue
is where your effort must go.*

Transformation

"The light! / the light stood before us / waiting! / I thought the world / stood still."
William Carlos Williams, "Asphodel, That Greeny Flower"

One of the most disorienting things about getting married was that I didn't feel transformed after the ceremony. I had expected (and hoped!) to feel wiser, more enlightened about what lay ahead. Instead we sat in the rented limo holding hands and saying, "We did it!" as though what had taken place had not quite penetrated us.

It had, but so deeply and subtly that we didn't notice at first. Perhaps that's why so many cultures celebrate marriage with intense ritual. You need the line of demarcation of a new life clearly and deeply drawn. It takes a while to realize that although no special wisdom or other observable trait was conferred along with the marriage blessing, the two of you are irrevocably embarked on a journey unprecedented in your lives. That's why we need the marriage ceremony: to set in motion the tectonic shifts within.

❧

Marriage is a transformation of our spirit.
In this way it's truly a sacrament: an outward
and visible sign of an inward and spiritual grace.

Defining Partnership

"The greatest thing in the world is to know how to belong to oneself."
Michel Eyquem de Montaigne, *Essays*

When you marry, people's assumptions about "coupledom" kick in full force. Some will expect the two of you to be practically joined at the hip, rarely making plans apart. Others will complain if you don't spend enough time with them, separate from your spouse. This dilemma hits at the root question of who you are separately and together in your marriage, how you create your identity as an individual within a union.

You and your partner have your own expectations about partnership. Perhaps one of you insists on time alone with friends and the other feels left out. The balance here must change as your needs change. If too much separate socializing is going on, it could be a sign that one of you is feeling overwhelmed by the "together forever" aspects of marriage. This is indeed a scary promise that we make, and a difficult one to contemplate. Conversely, if your friends never see you apart from each other, perhaps you need to consider why it seems so important to show up in the world as a couple.

∽∾

Like planets, you revolve around each other in distinct but related orbits. Finding the balance that keeps you together but separate is a delicate process. Be patient with yourselves, and don't let others pressure you.

The Main Event

"Blouaugh! (feed/me)."
William Carlos Williams, "The Sea-Elephant"

Marriage is different from living together, a friend of mine observed, because "everyone relaxes." Often we take that to mean negative things: everyone drops their best behavior and starts to show their bad habits. That certainly happens. But it's also true that once you relax, you become more real, more genuine in every respect. More of you is available for your partner to learn about and wonder at. The tense longings and bottomless expectations of courtship fall away. You have gotten what you wanted. Now, no longer "wishing," you're "doing." A hardy, lusty realism replaces wide-eyed adoration. You get loose, ready for anything. You're an athlete, tuned up for the main event.

The familiarity and certainty that come with marriage
bring strength for the journey inward.

Chemistry

"The color of the ground was in him, the red earth, /
The smack and tang of elemental things."
Edwin Markham, *Lincoln, The Man of the People*

I love the smell of my husband's skin and hair; the shadows we become, folded together at night. Then I inhale him, clinging to his back like a sailor to the mast. Our partner is our biological opposite. There is something alien and invigorating about him. Enjoy his strangeness. Soak up his hot energy. Gather it like treasures sunk in warm sand.

You and your husband are chemical.
Exchange your elements.

Your Past, Your Present

"One-woman waterfall, she wears / Her slow descent like a long cape /
And pausing, on the final stair / Collects her motions into shape."

X. J. Kennedy, "Nude Descending a Staircase"

The passion to get a new marriage off on the right foot is consuming. It can exhibit itself in an intense period of nesting, during which you forgo many of the activities you pursued as a single person. This is natural: Your energies are being poured into creating your identity as a couple. You may have gone too far in this direction, however, if you find yourself thinking: "It's been so long since I —————." Marriage is a powerful process that we rightly sense is one of the most important endeavors we'll ever undertake. Yet part of the task is to integrate your past life with your present one, not just to throw your former self overboard. Selecting and slowly introducing into your marriage activities and habits you pursued in your single years is the real work of forging a union of two separate souls. It is a workmanlike process, sometimes filled with friction. It has none of the balmlike bliss of the early days. But the reward is a seamlessness, an ability to move back and forth between your old and new selves, that is immeasurably rich.

The person you were and the person you are must come together
in marriage. Otherwise you will feel dislocated within it.

Lip Service

"Anyone can hold the helm when the sea is calm."

Publilius Syrus, Maxim 358

I used to think that being supportive meant always being nice, approving, laudatory. Now I know that it has more to do with truth telling than with praise giving. I am the only person who can tell my husband when he's full of shit—and survive the process. He trusts that I won't insult his intelligence by telling him what he wants to hear, but will honor him with what he *needs* to hear.

Confronting is a good thing, when it is done lovingly. The other person must sense your wish to help him handle a bad situation, not to hurt him or to vindicate yourself at his expense.

∽

Few people in our lives care enough about us to risk telling us the unvarnished truth when it would most help us to hear it. Put your love in the service of honesty.

The Comfort of Being Known

"Of all mad matches never was the like."
William Shakespeare, *The Taming of the Shrew*

Settle down, babe," my husband admonishes during one of my aimless fits of temper. Miraculously, I do. Anyone else even considering calling me "babe," much less telling me to "settle down," would be struck dead in his tracks. But my husband says it with such love that he gets away with it.

No one can rile me like my husband, but no one can calm me as he does either. "We're all looking for our Petruchio," a friend once remarked. She was referring not to a man who would tame us but to one who so deeply understood us that he could stand in the path of our rages and hold us in the storm of our tears. Such a man isn't interested in taming but meets us squarely on every level of who we are.

❧

Isn't it amazing how well you know how to handle each other?
Isn't it interesting that you allow each other to do so?

No More Searching

"*We make ourselves a place apart / Behind light words that tease and flout, /*
But oh, the agitated heart / Till someone really find us out."

Robert Frost, "Revelation"

We live near several bars that attract a singles crowd on weekends. I often walk past them on my way home. It is always the same scene: women and men dressed with careful attention, eyeing each other with studied indifference. All young, with the tight bodies and quick, nervous look of too many hours at a health club; too much unanswered ambition; not enough love in their lives. I feel lucky to know that that world is not mine to come home to. A man is waiting for me and I for him. I gladly accept the responsibilities of monogamy in exchange for its many luxuries, chief among which is needing to look no further to find my heart's true love.

Relax. Enjoy. You have come home.

How You Dreamed It Would Be

"But there's nothing half so sweet in life / As love's young dream."
Clement Clark Moore, "Love's Young Dream"

We begin marriage filled with dreams. At first there is only the dream. Then the reality of marriage consumes us. It's easy to get lost in the maze of day-to-day survival, losing sight of the ideals we held at the start. Don't be swayed from your dreams and aspirations. Staying in touch with your dreams gives you a framework for shaping each detail of daily life. Without dreams, marriage becomes a collection of grunts and groans; a scrapbook of grievances; a formless space.

⁌⁍

Take time to recall the hopes that birthed your life together.
Let them help you place your hand wisely in the midst of conflict.

Honesty

"Never go to bed mad. Stay up and fight."
Phyllis Diller, *Phyllis Diller's Housekeeping Hints*

When I was first married, I got into the habit of going out for a walk when an argument left me feeling frustrated and upset. I figured that this would help me cool off. It worked—too well. I'd walk until I had wound down enough to contain my rage in a neat little box deep within. Then I would go back and apologize. It felt so grown-up. Only later, when the fury sprang up faster than before and we'd be at it over something else, did I realize that I was misusing this strategy to stuff down my anger. Instead of saying what had to be said, I fled. Sometimes you've just got to hang in there and have it out. Or spend some time alone getting to the bottom of the rage and then go back and share what you found under all that murk. That is a disciplined use of anger. Evasion is unhealthy—and futile.

⟋⟍

*If you're flaring up a lot, something's going on
that needs your attention. Instead of walking it off,
have the courage to face it with your partner
and the faith that you'll work it out.*

The Gifts You Bring

*"O love is the crooked thing, / There is nobody wise enough /
To find out all that is in it."*
William Butler Yeats, "Brown Penny"

Each of you brings different skills to your marriage. The way he thinks of wonderful new activities to do, bringing adventure into your life together ... the way you think of interesting things to say, creating adventures in your mutual emotional journey. The way he is better at tying up newspapers for recycling than at getting good reception on channel 4, which is your domain. The way he selects imaginative gifts ... the way you write poignant letters that keep you both in touch with friends far away. The way he stays up with you when you're sick ... the magical massages you give at the end of a difficult day. There is a beautiful complementarity between you, each of you contributing your gifts to create a fully rounded whole.

*None of us loves alike.
That is what makes it all so interesting.*

Chosen

"*All women are not Helen, / I know that, / but have Helen in their hearts. /
My sweet, / you have it also, therefore / I love you.*"

William Carlos Williams, "Asphodel, That Greeny Flower"

There's a sense of awe that this person really wants to hang out with you," a friend observed about her marriage. Just as you have chosen your spouse, so he has chosen you. Remembering what an honor this is can help you to remain worthy of having been chosen. The exact reasons why you have been chosen will always remain something of a mystery—who can truly untangle the web of physical attraction, intellectual allure, and raw emotional need that causes one person to desire another? This essential mystery is good: It keeps us honing all our angles, shining all our surfaces—for who knows which facets we can afford to let dull?

✺

*Let the mystery of your partner's attraction to
you spur you to be your best self.*

Much Is Asked; Much Is Given

"When you first were married, your ring looked so obvious and new.
Now it's as if you've grown into your ring and your ring has grown into you."

A Friend

Marriage calls for every ounce of maturity we have. It also offers a stage for every childish mood and tantrum. Don't be surprised if you find yourself seesawing through these emotions, feeling a wonderful calm unity one moment and the chaotic urge to scream and slam doors the next. Marriage challenges you to put into play everything you know. It demands every survival skill you possess—and many you don't yet possess. Growing into your marriage is an exhilarating challenge to the spirit.

❧

You have taken on a large and noble task. You own it,
and it owns you. You can never be shaken loose
from the transformation that has occurred.

Consideration

"Never . . . be mean in anything; never be false; never be cruel."
Charles Dickens, *David Copperfield*

Recently my husband came home several hours after I had expected him. I had long since passed through puzzlement, peevishness, fury, and worry and had entered a state of abject terror. Seeing my wild expression, he looked sheepish. "I was in a bookstore and lost track of time," he confessed.

There is a basic level of courtesy in marriage that often must be learned through situations much like this one. Letting the other person know where you are or that you're running late smooths the path of marriage. Courtesy shows us that we are valued, thought about, and cared for.

∽∾

*Courtesies are a simple way to let our partner know
how much their contentment means to us.*

The Work of Time

"Surely these things lie on the knees of the gods."
Homer, *The Odyssey*

When I first began dating my husband, our arguments always had to be settled right away—within hours—or I'd be frantic with pain and impatience. After we'd been going out a year or so, the time frame lengthened: We sometimes took days to settle things. Now that we're married, our sense of time seems to have expanded again. I don't think of our arguments as crises that must be resolved. I think of our life as an unfolding process.

Marriage changes our notion of time. We have a lifetime to spend together—and we begin to realize that not everything can be handled quickly and decisively. Agreements are struck; then they mutate; then they are re-formed in yet another configuration as time and life re-form us. Some issues are let go of altogether. Some arise that would have been unthinkable a few years earlier. And some never get resolved.

∽

Letting problems go unsolved doesn't mean you're getting lazy.
You've learned that some problems untangle only in their own time.

Disciples

"What you don't know would make a great book."
Sydney Smith, *Lady Holland's Memoir*

Y ou have many things to teach each other. I'm talking not about phi-
losophy here but actual skills: how to roast a chicken; shoot baskets;
secure a loan; tend a campfire. Let yourselves be beginners with each
other, absorbing skills the other can teach. There is a wonderful intimacy in
surrendering your total attention to each other in this way, rediscovering each
other's unique wisdom.

*Become learners again. Honor each
other with the attentive openness of the student.*

Separation

"We must have richness of soul."
Antiphanes, *Greek Comic Fragments*

It's important to put some air into the marriage. That means getting away from each other now and then. For some people, a night out alone or with friends does the trick. For some it takes a week solo in the Bahamas or London. Others may think this is strange at best; a sign of trouble at worst. So long as you both agree that nothing of the kind is afoot, what does it matter what anyone else thinks? Missing each other and coming home with stories to share enables you to meet and fall in love all over again.

❧

In the calm space of solitude, the wish for union is restored.

Changing Each Other

"Even if you persuade me, you won't persuade me."
Aristophanes, *Plutus*

"I don't care. I will never care. And I don't care that I don't care!" This was my response to my husband's pleas to sort the laundry into whites and colors. Undoubtedly my husband feels this way about a number of things I'd like him to do. The lesson here is that some things we will change; some things we'll willingly work on changing, and many things we absolutely, positively will not change. Sometimes we just do what we do, and to hell with anyone else's opinion. Change can happen only with our permission. We don't change for other people. We change for ourselves. If your partner changes for you but not for himself, he'll resent you for it. So you haven't "won" a thing— you'll just think you have.

Don't waste time trying to get each other to change.
Battle over the biggies if you have to, but let most of it go.
Change, if it's going to happen, will take its own time.

Friends

*"The people people have for friends / Your common sense appall, /
But the people people marry / Are the queerest folk of all."*
Charlotte Perkins Gilman, "Queer People"

You do not have to like each other's friends. You also do not have to tell each other so. You both know the ones you're lukewarm about. Remember that you're spending your lives with each other, not with each other's friends. Instead of looking at what his choice of friends may say about his flaws, look at what choosing you says about his strengths.

❧

*In our selection of others, we show many of our own qualities.
In choosing you, what has your partner revealed?*

Single Friends

"True friendship is never serene."

Marie de Rabutin-Chantal, Marquise de Sévigné, *Lettres,* "Madame de Grignon"

Once you marry, some of your single friends may find it hard to be around you. It may be painful for them to see you happy with your mate. Perhaps it reminds them of the longed-for intimacy that they do not have. You'll find it difficult to connect with them, and this will distress you. Recognize that they must come to terms with this in their own time. Try to stay connected in any way you can, and don't take their withdrawal personally. If it happens that this friendship does not survive, understand that the parting is as sad for your friend as it is for you.

○∽○

Friendships change and sometimes evaporate,
with or without marriage. Acceptance can be your
only path here, with the hope that it may lead,
in time, to reconciliation.

What About Money?

"The guinea is yours; and the guinea is a free gift, given freely."
Virginia Woolf, *Three Guineas*

Money, like sex, brings out interesting behavior in people. The best way to deal with the money issue is to agree to do whatever you must do in order not to fight about it. Money matters need to be articulated in that treatylike spirit: "Look, I want things to feel fair to us both." Don't let disputes ride or ignore signs of trouble. Work at them gently and carefully until you reach a resolution both of you can live with. For some that may mean keeping everything separate and splitting expenses right down the middle. For others it may mean merging accounts completely. For many of us it means some combination of the two. This is a murky place, where we may see our own wishes more clearly than our partner's needs—with the necessities within the marriage being murkier still.

Take money matters one step at a time.
Change in this area often needs to be incremental,
and always respectful.

Allow for Anger

"A disagreement may be the shortest cut between two minds."
Kahlil Gibran, *Sand and Foam*

We're often told that we should express, express, express our anger to our partner, rooting out discords as they arise. When our anger persists, we feel we have failed. Don't expect to walk around free of anger at your partner. You know too much about each other, good and bad. You have history, good and bad. Intimacy couldn't exist without that knowledge. If anger cannot flow freely in your relationship, you will never be able to go very deep with your partner—you won't be able to withstand the emotional pressures involved.

Instead of thinking that you and your partner must always forgive each other, why not forgive your anger instead? Understand that it's there because you and your partner are close, and closeness steps on toes, isn't cute, is often messy. Let your anger teach you so it won't rule you, shouting for attention. Let the spectrum of your marriage be big enough to hold anger.

The sure way to lose Eden is to pay too much attention to the serpent. But even Eden had a serpent.

Creating Traditions

"And on the table / one fried fish / spattered with burning scarlet sauce, /
a little dish / of hominy grits / and four pink tissue-paper roses."
Elizabeth Bishop, *"Jerónimo's House"*

Forging your own traditions is an important statement—both to yourselves and to your families. It lets everyone know that a new family exists in the world that hadn't existed before. This sometimes needs reinforcement, polite but repeated. It's easy for your families to assume that holidays will be celebrated the same as always, for example. It's up to you to make your own assertions in this area. It helps to be gentle and matter-of-fact and not to wait until the last minute to announce your plans or evolving thoughts on the subject. Ease your relatives into the realization that the two of you now are answerable to each other and that it's more important for you and your partner to be in accord than for you to do the things others approve of. You need to do this gradually, because it helps to be humane rather than harsh and divisive—and because you may need these gentle reminders as much as others do.

∽

Creating a new identity as a couple is an incremental process.
Everyone needs time to adjust. Go slowly, but don't let others ignore the
fundamental shift in priorities and accountability that has taken place.

Grown Together

"So I can't live either without you or with you."
Ovid, *Amores*

One gets to this point quickly in marriage: We can't conceive of life without our partner, but the idea of spending the rest of our days with this collection of bumps, bruises, bad habits, and odd attitudes seems equally unthinkable. It is a strange position that asks us to live two mutually exclusive points of view. Somehow we rise to the occasion, which is a testament to the deep character marriage calls forth from us. We take the bumps because we know the glory that lives behind them. We take the glory when it comes and live on the memory of it during dark days.

∾

Marriage asks us to contemplate "forever" as a way of life.
It is a world without end of our own creation.

Growth

"Love knows nothing of order."
Saint Jerome

Marriage grows jaggedly. My husband and I enjoy months of serenity, followed by weeks where every comment seems to spark an argument. It appears we must go through periods when, like clothes we outgrow, we don't "fit" each other and must remake the mantle of our marriage. Or maybe we are like the glacier cutting through granite: We exert on each other a constant, primordial pressure, grinding a new landscape for ourselves.

Marriage is a natural force set in motion. Its growth, uneven and ill timed, carries its own inexorable logic: When we are strong enough and ready, we are compelled to stretch, flex, and demand the room our new selves require.

❦

*Marriage changes as we change. The process
is like any natural phenomenon—uneven, unpredictable,
relentless. Take the surges as they come.*

Being There, Getting There

*"If you should put even a little on a little, and should do
this often, soon this too would become big."*

Hesiod, *Works and Days*

Sitting around a picnic table with friends, my husband and I feel like babes in the woods: One couple has been married for seventeen years; the other is working on thirty. At a year and counting, getting to five or ten seems worthy of some kind of award. The years pass so quickly, our friends tell us; time goes faster and faster. The clichés run past us, meaningless. Our friends have no secrets to offer, no success formulas. They don't really know how they got as far as they have, any more than we know how we'll get there. "One thing about your father," my mother once told me, "is that he's always there." Willingness counts as much as wisdom, it seems, in the enduring marriage.

*Sometimes the secret of the game lies in just
showing up, day after day, ready to play.*

The Real Thing

"There is much to be said for failure. It is more interesting than success."
Max Beerbohm, "Mainly on the Air"

With marriage comes much talk by both partners about partnership. Concurrently, powerful individual agendas are being pushed, right alongside our truly genuine desire for oneness. It's a rich irony, a paradox that few of us can admit. Yet being able to see that you are only human in this way can relieve a lot of the pressure to "do marriage" perfectly. Once perfection has been jettisoned, you are free to shape a reality that truly works for the two of you. Creativity can blossom in the vacuum left by failed expectations. And therein lies another paradox of marriage: giving up the dream of perfection gives you entry to an Eden of your own making.

⌒⌒

Give up the stasis of "perfect partners" and take up the journey of "struggling lovers." See the new places you can go.

Doing Too Much

"It is better to be hated for what you are than loved for what you are not."
André Gide

I am sitting in the laundromat while our clothes tumble in the spin cycle. I'm about to squeeze a trip to the grocery store in between insertions of quarters, detergent, more quarters, and fabric softener. I'm drinking a cup of take-out coffee and wolfing down a muffin. And I'm writing this entry.

What blessed primordial gene is it that enables women to do six things at once while keeping a lookout for the saber-toothed tiger lurking somewhere down the path? We are the world's great organizers and doers. Yet sometimes this capability runs rampant. When it does, it runs our life—literally.

Marriage can kick this gene into high gear. We need to monitor ourselves carefully, resisting the urge to take care of too many things at once. Our spouse got along quite well without us for decades; what makes us think we are so indispensable to him now? This lesson is one that keeps having to be learned.

❧

Stop gyrating. You are enough, just as you are.

Forgive Yourself

"I am simply a human being, more or less."
Saul Bellow, *Herzog*

Y ou've done something wrong. Said something wrong. Things are bad, and it's your fault. Have some compassion for yourself. You can admit your mistakes without beating yourself up over them. For-giving yourself gives you the space to acknowledge the part you played in creating the problem, and the mental freedom to invent a way out of chaos.

You do many things right each day, but you're going to make mistakes sometimes. You certainly don't expect perfect behavior from your spouse. Think of the allowances you make and realize that he's probably making them for you, too. Be strong enough to admit your faults, apologize if that's neces-sary, and move on.

∾

Your marriage can tolerate a tremendous
amount of strain. Have faith that it can contain
your flaws. Use its elasticity as a model
for self-acceptance.

Live It, Don't Watch It

"No thing great is created suddenly, any more than a bunch of grapes or a fig.
If you tell me that you desire a fig, I answer you that there must be time.
Let it first blossom, then bear fruit, then ripen."

Epictetus, *Discourses*

I used to remember every significant date related to our courtship and marriage: six months of dating; one year of dating; monthly milestones of our engagement; and so on. Wandering in a churchyard in Bailey's Island, Maine, the day after we were married, I looked at my watch at 3:20 P.M. and recalled that exactly twenty-four hours earlier, we had exchanged vows.

Nowadays I often forget these landmarks. This worried me at first. I thought I was becoming jaded. In fact, what's happening is that when we marry, we're no longer on the monthly/yearly plan; we're on the decade plan. The new landmarks in our lives are measured in large chunks of time: thirty-year mortgages, decades until retirement; silver and golden anniversaries. We become too caught up in living the marriage to spend much time observing its milestones. When we feel secure, we don't have to note the passing of every tranquil hour or count each goal attained.

The time line of your life is unfolding on a different level now.
Celebrate your new ability to meet time on expanded terms.

Peace

"As soon as you trust yourself, you will know how to live."
Johann Wolfgang von Goethe, *Faust*

An even keel is a tempting thing. In our relationship, we sometimes keep the peace for the sake of maintaining an ideal image—public or private. We also may do it because we're too tired, too sad, too angry to know what else to do. So we shut up and go along to get along. The result may be welcome silence in the house, but there's often a clamor within. The next time you are tempted to steer toward an even keel, think about your *inner* silence: What would it take to achieve that? Commitment to inner silence might be the way to achieve peace at home.

❧

The quality of your inner silence is the source of all your offerings in your marriage. Seek the contentment your soul requires.

Comradeship

*"So we grew together, / Like to a double cherry, seeming parted, /
But yet an union in partition; / Two lovely berries molded on one stem."*
Shakespeare, *A Midsummer Night's Dream*

If we are healthy people, we are independent people. Particularly if we've been single for a while before getting married, we have gotten very good at acting unilaterally. After all, when we were single, if we didn't take care of it/decide it/do it, who would? I am always shocked, then, when I come home and trot out my latest decisive action, and my spouse not only tells me in great detail why he thinks it's a lousy decision but also demands to know why he wasn't consulted. It would be inappropriate, of course, to check in on every question. But bear in mind that there is another person in the equation who is just as independent as you are. And, if *he* is healthy, he will want a say in the choices affecting his life. Collaboration can be a great comfort, if only we could remember to do it!

❧

*You're going to be held accountable for things no
one challenged you about before—but you don't have
to make all the decisions alone anymore.*

Busyness

"No human thing is of serious importance."
Plato, *The Republic*

Does it seem as if you're always running, doing, planning, talking? There's much to plan and to accomplish in life. But busyness can block true understanding of your partner. It's easier to ask, "What are we doing about dinner?" or say, "You won't believe what happened at work today!" than it is to ask your partner whether he's happy with himself; whether he's happy with you.

Sit quietly together. What is the quality of the silences between you? Do you screen each other out? Feel companionable? Feel restless? Perhaps you'll use his listening presence to tell him you're glad to see him rather than to voice a complaint about the day. Maybe he'll tell you about a fear he can barely admit to himself. Don't let daily static divert you from quiet moments together.

$\backsim$

In the fabric of silence, a common dream is woven.

Relatives

"Criticism comes easier than craftsmanship."
Pliny the Elder, *Natural History*

Relatives—yours and his—are not to be used as ammunition. They are not to use you as ammunition. You and your husband must agree on these two basic principles, or your marriage will be ruled by your ties to your family of origin instead of by your sworn bond to each other. Resist the urge to psychoanalyze your in-laws. Your husband will not thank you for your insights. These are things it is his job to learn. It also is not loving or respectful to your in-laws.

If you enjoy your in-laws, tell them so, often and wholeheartedly. If you don't enjoy your in-laws, a charitable attitude is less corrosive to all concerned. It is sad that they don't know any other way to be; that they don't have the relief of feeling open, trusting, loving. This doesn't make their actions less infuriating, but it may help you find the compassion you need to maintain your humanity and goodwill.

*Feeling upset, suspicious, and defensive stresses you
more than anyone else. Why allow anyone that power?*

Autonomy

"Different we are, as facts have proved, both in sex and in education.
And it is from that difference . . . that our help can come. . . ."

Virginia Woolf, *Three Guineas*

Sometimes I find myself asking my husband his views about things and feeling that I should adjust my views accordingly. Our society reinforces the idea that married people are a unit with one mind. It's only natural that we occasionally fall into the habit of forgetting ourselves; forgetting that we once decided all by ourselves on clothes and haircut styles and whether or not we needed to take an umbrella when we went out. These minutiae may seem insignificant, but taken together they create the body of ideas, preferences, opinions, and idiosyncrasies that give us form in the world. It's not a far journey from these to the deeper questions of identity, ethics, dreams, and ambitions that should be no one's province but our own. Don't get into the habit of giving away the small stuff, or you may find the big stuff slipping away, too.

Certain decisions should be yours and yours alone,
without explanation or apology.

Tolerance

"You cannot teach a crab to walk straight."
Aristophanes, *Peace*

There are some household chores my husband just won't do. He appears to have a permanent impairment when it comes to cleaning the toilet, for example. But I am incurable when it comes to my habit, while cooking, of licking the spoon and sticking it back in the pot. We all come to a point in marriage where we recognize that there are certain things our partner just won't do. It's not about sexism, laziness, or deep flaws in character (although in the heat of the moment, I have been known to doubt this). It's just about accepting the immutability of idiosyncrasy. Give it up, both of you. Let the other guy be.

❧

Your partner's quirks of character are hard-wired from babyhood. They are not calculated affronts to you. Try not to take them personally.

Generosity

"I shall have to learn a little greek to keep up with this / but so will you, drratt you."
Ezra Pound, "Canto CV"

Are you able to be close to your partner on *his* terms? Perhaps it wouldn't be your choice to sit in a stadium in subzero weather watching heavily padded men do serious injury to one another over a pigskin-covered object. Perhaps it isn't his idea of heaven to dress up and talk for two hours over a candlelit dinner that neither of you had to prepare. No matter. The question is, Are you both willing to do these things anyway?

෧෧

Your partner's idea of intimacy may be
vastly different from yours. Try it his way, and
keep an open mind. Honor his idea of closeness
as you wish him to honor yours.

Isolation

"To know that you do not know is the best.
To pretend to know when you do not know is a disease."

Lao-tzu, *The Way of Lao-tzu*

When it comes to marriage, lots of people have advice, but few have wisdom. It's as though after the vows are taken, a curtain descends, and each person's experience of marriage becomes the most private of secrets. People are plenty willing to tell you what's "right" and "normal." Few, however, will admit to the dismay and confusion that marriage throws us into: the doubts, the sense of floundering toward solutions. To hear of these struggles would be to hear wisdom. We know we must find our own answers. We simply seek the reassurance that others, too, struggle. Many are reluctant to admit this, yet it would be the greatest comfort to know. In this way our culture makes islands of us all.

❧

When we feel that everyone else is doing OK and
we aren't, we become isolated and discouraged. In fact,
everyone struggles, and you are not alone.

He's Not the Enemy

"Couples are wholes and not wholes, what agrees disagrees, the concordant is discordant. From all things one and from one all things."

Heraclitus, *On the Universe*

When you are in conflict with your partner, it's natural to think of him as the enemy: he's at odds with you. In fact, this person is on your side. He's on your team. If he's angry or upset, maybe it's because he's trying hard to get the team to work better, not simply to push his own agenda. Don't forget that he, too, has a vested interest in seeing the marriage work.

Experiment with holding the awareness that you and your partner are working from common ground—wanting the marriage to "win"—and that if he's yelling at you, he's doing it the way a teammate would chastise another teammate who keeps letting the ball slip past him so the other side scores. Maybe if you agree to practice your punt, he'll admit that he needs to work on his forward pass.

❦

Try assuming that your husband is on your side, and observe the differences it makes in defusing the power of conflict at home.

How You Fit

"The union of hands and hearts."
Jeremy Taylor, "The Marriage Ring"

In the musical *1776*, John Adams and Benjamin Franklin conspire to bring Thomas Jefferson's new wife to Philadelphia, because lack of newlywed sex is giving the architect of our Declaration of Independence a horrific case of writer's block. As the reunited pair stand locked in an embrace, Adams nudges Franklin, worrying that they might have gotten hold of the wrong woman and that perhaps these two aren't really married. "Of course they are," Franklin chuckles. "Look how they fit."

How do you "fit" with your partner? Do you fall into step together? Does your head have a special niche in the hollow of his shoulder? Do you finish what's on each other's plates—or each other's sentences? Look for these signs of unity between you. It's fun to notice them together. They are a sweet, small way to affirm your bond.

Enjoy your fitting-together.
Take your oneness wherever you find it.

No More "Nice Girl"

"The bow too tensely strung is easily broken."
Publilius Syrus, Maxim 388

A wise colleague once told me, "Don't get too good at jobs you don't really want to do." The same goes for marriage. It's tempting to be the perfect, willing spouse, doing all sorts of tasks you hate, to show that you're a good sport. This is part of what we were taught as "nice girls" at home and "team players" at work. But it can run you into trouble. Always being the first to jump up and clear the table after dinner—when what you'd really like is to sit and enjoy the rest of your glass of wine—is a sure path to resentment of the fact that your husband, naturally, will begin to expect this behavior from you. You discover that the job that you pitched in to do just to be helpful ends up defining you, not the other way around. Do you find yourself doing things in your marriage that you wouldn't even have considered doing when you were single!? If so, it's time to break the pattern. Make a conscious effort to refrain from those jobs—and resist the urge to polish your skills at other tasks you don't really care if you ever get good at.

❧

*Be careful that your urge to
rescue situations doesn't put you at risk.*

Solitude

"Those who dream by day are cognizant of many things
which escape those who dream only by night."

Edgar Allan Poe, *Eleanora*

When we are married, it is easy to become more a partner than a person. Find a place where you can rediscover yourself in solitude: a place where you can think, dwell, or dream uninterrupted. Make a point of going there on a regular basis, away from your connection with work, home, colleagues, partner. In this quiet space, stay a minute or two past the point when you think it's time to leave. Persist in lengthening the amount of time you allow yourself to be alone, with nothing of any consequence to do.

∽

Sometimes leaving the relationship
is the best way to remain within it.

Hidden Agendas

"Once harm has been done, even a fool understands it."
Homer, *The Iliad*

My partner just can't take encouragement," a friend complained. This was puzzling. Lots of people can't take criticism, but who doesn't crave encouragement? Sometimes, however, we offer our partner criticism cleverly disguised as encouragement. The disguise fools even us, and so we are dismayed and affronted when our partner rejects our well-meant words.

If your attempt at support ends in an argument, chances are your partner is hearing a hidden subtext implying that his efforts somehow fell short of the mark. His anger stems from his sense that suddenly *your* standards have become the measure of his deeds, and *he* has been lost in the process. You may find it difficult to attune yourself to these instances because your words probably are coming from a very sincere place. Still, you need to tune in to your own subtext and ask yourself why you've decided that what your partner has accomplished isn't enough.

❧

True praise comes with no strings attached.

Doing Nothing

"That indolent but agreeable condition of doing nothing."
Pliny the Younger, *Letters*

Take time to hang out together. Otherwise you may forget how. In the busy world we hit headlong every day, doing nothing is a skill that needs cultivating. If you've gone for a long time without doing nothing, it will seem strange at first. You'll twitch and flit; get up and sit down; start to talk and stop again. Just sit with your restlessness and be patient. When it passes, you'll be able to find pure companionship, free of the frenzied romantic energy of the early days, before life together habituated you to each other.

Sit and do nothing together.
More than talking, it will put you back in sync.

Keeping Secrets

"My strength is as the strength of ten, / Because my heart is pure."
Tennyson, *Sir Galahad*

Keeping secrets is the fastest way to knock the props from under your marriage. I'm not talking about harmless secrets—the white lies that enable people to live together unencumbered by the burden of petty hurts. I'm talking about bad behavior that is deliberately hidden; resentments allowed to fester. If you practice the discipline of continually coming clean with your partner, you can push back the boundaries of trust so each of you can contain more of the other's "unmentionable" secrets, snits, idiocies, grudges, jealousies, and general nuttiness about life. What would be so bad about honoring your partner by letting him see you naked this way, with all your ugly secrets hanging out? Your honesty gives your best self room to come forward.

❦

Begin a daily practice of telling a secret to your partner.

Tuning In

"Truth is great and its effectiveness endures."
Ptahhotpe, *The Maxims of Ptahhotpe*

An old "husband-catching" lesson used to be, "Ask him about himself." A woman was supposed to lasso a man's heart by massaging his ego. What retro hogwash, we scoff. But if it's hogwash, why do I find that my learning about the punts and penalties of football and my husband's learning about the jumps and jetés of ballet draw us closer and make both of us happy? Here's the key: It's not about *subordinating your interests* to his; it's about *taking an interest* in the things that light him up. Be sure your interest is real and not feigned. If you will never love football, don't suffer in silence. Your partner will smell your falseness eventually, and this corrodes all trust. But if you feel you can come to appreciate the desperate beauty of a Hail Mary pass, why not say so?

❧

Taking a genuine interest in your partner's life
is one of the simplest ways to show your love.

Stop Helping

> *"One must not always think so much about what one should do, but rather what one should be."*
>
> Meister Eckhart, *Work and Being*

You are not your partner's keeper. It is not your responsibility to see that he gets to work on time, has clean shirts, finds his socks, or buys gifts for his family's birthdays. As women, it's easy to fall into the trap of thinking it's our responsibility to handle all the things that no one else appears to care about—until, of course, they discover that *you* haven't done them!

The habit of overnurturance can be painful to break. There will be cries of, "Why didn't you . . . ?" and "You should have . . . !" Hold firm and respond reasonably: "Now, why should you assume that I would remember your sister's birthday when you didn't?"

No one learns anything by having their life lived for them. You're doing your partner no favors by doing too much. A favor is a one-time act that you willingly undertake—and that your spouse recognizes as such. If you aren't hearing thank-yous, you aren't doing favors. And if you are feeling more angry and unappreciated than willing, your nurturing behaviors may need reining in.

$\backsim$

Are you taking better care of your partner's life than of your own?

Love and Laughter

"The body, she says, is subject to the forces of gravity. But the soul is ruled by levity, pure."
Saul Bellow, *Him with His Foot in His Mouth*

I'm getting in with you." My husband sticks one foot into the bath water. I start to giggle and then am speechless, fighting for air, elbow- and knee-space in our ancient bathtub, which is small enough to beach a minnow. Soon our romantic tryst is reduced to a bristle of limbs in a tepid puddle. "Fun," my husband mutters, his head wedged under the faucet.

It didn't matter. Laughter can be a great aphrodisiac—which is a good thing, since sex can be pretty laughable. And sometimes laughter is more available than steamy ardor, especially when the days are long and arduous. Waiting for the "perfect moment" will only keep you waiting. Take what you can get and give what you can give. Start now.

Love is too rare a thing to hoard.

Face the Music

very now and then partners bring us down to earth with a thud by telling us a truth about ourselves that makes us wince, squirm, or deny. When you find yourself mired in any of these behaviors, ask yourself if you are reacting so powerfully because a truth you don't want to admit is being revealed about you. What is so dangerous about examining it, turning it over like a puzzle in your hands? Admitting that he's right needn't come until later; you've got plenty of time to gather your courage for that. In the meantime, instead of lobbing a grenade into his camp, receive his comment with a sense of possibility: "That's interesting. I'll need some time to think about that."

❧

*You are going to hear some tough truths about yourself in the course
of your marriage. Why not use them to your advantage?*

Visions and Sightings

"The magic of a face."
Thomas Carew, "Epitaph on the Lady S----"

A strange thing happened today at the movies," my husband told me. "I was thinking about you, and suddenly I saw you in a whole new way. You literally looked different. You were like someone I'd never seen before, right there in the middle of *Journey to the Center of the Earth."*

I, too, have had this experience of seeing my partner anew, as if he were a stranger, compelling my interest. It's odd and unsettling but a wonderful trick of the mind that reveals, in a sort of vision, our partner's enduring mystery. It is a reminder of the essential unknowability of the person we married. It reignites our desire to plumb this stranger's depths. It reminds us that true knowledge of another hangs just out of reach, keeping us wondering. And that this is just as it should be.

☙

*The more you think you know your partner, the more elusive he becomes.
Dive deep and realize you will never touch bottom.*

Skin to Skin

*"And now good morrow to our waking souls, / Which watch not one another out of fear; /
For love, all love of other sights controls, / And makes one little room, an everywhere."*

John Donne, "The Good Morrow"

In the morning, before you get up, take time to touch each other. Let the day wait, all its busyness still before you, while you reacquaint yourselves with each other. There's no reason to snap to attention at the call of the clock. As soon as you swim up out of sleep, in that delicious pre-waking lethargy, make a new imprint of your lover upon your mind. Doing this reminds you that you are sustained by something greater than the daily whirlwind.

Restore each other with touch.

Open Heart

"And we forget because we must / And not because we will."
Matthew Arnold, *Absence*

Forgiveness doesn't mean you don't remember your hurts. It is a voluntary act, undertaken despite pain. In marriage you need to be bigger than your hurt inner child. Bigger than your raging ego.

Don't expect pain to go away. You must walk away. This is not the same as burying your hurts. True forgiveness is wholehearted and does not look back longingly. True forgiveness is a quiet voice that says, "Let us continue. Let us go on with our journey." It is easier to crouch in your dark tent than to set your feet on this path. But there is no way to find the next oasis if you won't cross the desert.

❧

Don't wait to feel in the mood to forgive. Take yourself in hand and set out toward the serenity you seek. Forgiveness is your choice to make.

The Promise of Pictures

"From their eyelids as they glanced dripped love."
Hesiod, *The Theogony*

I should look more often at my wedding pictures. Like most people, I get them out only to show others who ask to see them. But every time I turn the thick pages of that album and see our happy faces, the smiles of those who love us witnessing our vows, I am reconnected to the hope and passion that fuel marriage. It is all there in our faces—it's why so many people ask to see wedding photographs. It is always a comfort and an inspiration to recall that day of promises made, surrounded by those who raised us to the point where we could make them.

☙❧

Your marriage photos capture you at your most solemn, your most committed, your most ecstatic. Keep them where you can treasure them often.

Helping vs. Nagging

"Have I inadvertently said some evil thing?"
Phocion, *Plutarch, Apothegms*

My husband needs to lose a few pounds. I need to write this book. Each day we work at helping each other meet our many life goals. Sometimes, however, this "helping" crosses over into nagging. That doesn't work. It only makes the other person feel inadequate, beleaguered, and angry—like a child browbeaten by a parent—not exactly a climate where mature change can occur. It also puts you in the unwelcome position of living, doing, and breathing for your partner. You aren't helping by nagging or taking over. The best you can do is create a climate where change can happen. For me this means buying fewer sweet treats and refusing to turn food into a stress-reducing reward for myself and my spouse. It also means *not* rationing the sweets when we do have them. For my husband it means making quiet time available during which he encourages me to "go write epiphanies." It also means that he doesn't check up on whether I'm actually writing them or not.

*Give your partner the space to do his
own good. Then sit on your hands, bite your
tongue, and celebrate every small step.*

Be Puzzled

"Love is an endless mystery, for it has nothing else to explain it."
Rabindranath Tagore

D o you find yourself saying or thinking, "I know he'll say . . ." or "I know he wants . . ."? If so, you have fallen into the trap of letting the outcomes of the past rule the outcomes of the future. Thinking you know your partner is the fastest route to stagnation in marriage. There is no room for your transformation here; no freedom for growth, experimentation, or mystery. And mystery is where romance, interest, and sex all reside.

When you feel stale thinking overtake you, remind yourself that your partner is a stranger to you—a mysterious "other" with reactions and thoughts and values you have not even begun to tap. Don't assume that the lines of the play have already been written. Instead of saying, "I know what he'll think," *ask* him, "What do you think?" Give him a chance to reveal himself to you. Open yourself to the interest he holds.

❧

Asking your partner questions about
his thoughts and feelings is a kindness, for you
are honoring his fundamental mystery. You are saying,
"You are a puzzle. You intrigue me. I want to
see how all the pieces fit."

Have Fun

"Nothing like a little judicious levity."
Robert Louis Stevenson, *The Wrong Box*

Spend as much time as possible laughing with your partner. Look for funniness in life and share it with each other, even during difficult times. Shared happiness is the mortar that holds your house together. Mix humor into your marriage as consciously as you mix passion, insight, and judgment. Sometimes the only thing that gets you over a rough spot is a whistle or a smile.

☙

Laughter helps you give trouble the back of your hand.
Let it lighten your marriage.

"No."

"One says a lot in vain, refusing; / The other mainly hears the 'No.'"
Johann Wolfgang von Goethe, *Iphigenia in Tauris*

Think about how you say no to your partner. Do you say it in such a way that your partner can focus on the *why* behind the no? Are you able to say yes to *him* but no to the issue at hand? When the mind hears rejection, that rejection often fills consciousness completely, commanding all its attention. How would your articulation of *no* have to change in order to get your partner to hear something larger than refusal, something of potential rather than futility, in your words? It may feel good momentarily to be categorically negative, but if the ultimate goal is change, not simply the relief of stating your position, you may need to recast what you say and how you say it.

The word no *should open doors, not close them.*

Crack the Code

"Wha ha ha ha / Wheeeeee / Clacka tacka tacka / tacka tacka /
wha ha ha ha ha / ha ha ha"
William Carlos Williams, "The Trees"

Sometimes there's as much said between the lines as in the words themselves. When my husband is holed up in his studio, unable to bike home in bad weather, we talk on the phone before bed. Discussion about our arrogant, eccentric cat always ends the conversation: "Vinnie misses you something fierce," I say. "Oh, yeah?" my husband says, laughing. "He doesn't give a shit." "That's true," I say. From that little exchange we know who's really missing whom.

All couples have a love code that is understood only by them. Maybe it's a phrase coined during a significant struggle that never fails to bring a smile of shared recollection when repeated. Maybe it's a veiled reference that sends erotic awareness crackling between you. Whatever it is, it is kindling for intimacy that lives free of physical proximity, in the spaces between words.

Every couple has a love code. What is yours?

Stay Curious

Onne night I stayed late at work after two weeks of doing nothing but staying late at work. When I finally called my husband to tell him I was about to leave, it was with the knowledge that he had been expecting me more than an hour earlier. "Just come home," he said tersely. I did, filled with a noxious mixture of guilt for keeping him waiting and resentment that he was being so possessive of my time.

Not until a week later did I learn that I'd gotten it all wrong. He hadn't been angry *at* me; he'd been angry *for* me: He felt that lately I hadn't been setting aside enough time for myself.

In casting my partner as the selfish husband, I was selling him short while seeing myself as the martyred hero. The scary thing was, if I hadn't thought to ask a simple question—"Why did you sound so angry when you said that?" I never would have discovered his compassion.

The more convinced you are of what's going on with your partner,
the less you probably know. Never underestimate
the beauty and power of a direct question.

Insist on Being Indulged

Whim n. *A capricious or eccentric and often sudden idea or turn of the mind.*
Webster's New Collegiate Dictionary

"Why should I bring you flowers, when all they do is die?" This is how my husband responds when I tell him that I think it's fun to receive flowers. He probably will never understand what it is about flowers that I love. I don't understand it myself, except that it has something to do with glorious color and blissful self-indulgence. Understanding your partner's whims is beside the point. The point is that *you indulge them even though you don't understand them.* You have whims that deserve to be indulged. Whims aren't designed to be in agreement with anyone's opinions. They may not make sense even to you. They're unexplainable by definition! Impress upon your partner that you want him to give you flowers (or serve you breakfast in bed or buy you stupid stuffed toys or frilly underwear or whatever) for no other reason than that you want him to. Let him know that you will indulge his whims as well, not trying to talk him out of them. After all, who said that everything about us had to make sense?

Having your whims indulged feels important because it signifies your lover's unconditional acceptance of you. Don't feel guilty about asking to have your whims met. Don't forget to return the favor!

Best Friends, Worst Enemies

*"Stand your ground. Don't fire unless fired upon,
but if they mean to have a war let it begin here!"*
John Parker (to his Minutemen at Lexington, Massachusetts)

Trite as it may seem, my husband and I have become best friends. So when we argue, an odd thing happens: Because we always confide our troubles to each other, we feel unnerved and fearful when anger makes us withdraw into silence. Just when we're in the thick of not speaking to each other, we have the greatest impulse to confide in the very person with whom we're locked in combat. This urge becomes our greatest compulsion toward making up.

When you're arguing, you'll probably use your deep knowledge of your partner as a weapon. Be sure, as well, to use all you know about his friendship to move toward reconciliation.

෬෧

*Your best friend is also your craftiest, most persistent enemy.
This is one of the practical jokes of marriage.*

Running the Same Race

"At last the Dodo said, 'Everybody has won, and all must have prizes.'"
Lewis Carroll, *Alice in Wonderland*

My husband is a high-energy guy: up 'til the small hours; waking the next morning bright-eyed and sharp-witted. I am slower, needful of sleep, seeking "down time" in which to think, dream, and muddle through problems. We have had to learn to respect each other's very different ways of going about life. Expecting him to slow down and enter my misty world, or me to enter his electric one, would only disorient us both. We have found that when left to our own devices, each of us ends up in the same place, starting from different points. And the insights we bring from the landscape of our peculiar journeys enrich each other beyond measure.

∽◦᷅

You are never as wise alone as you are together.

Come Clean

"Truths kindle light for truths."
Lucretius, *De Rerum Natura*

Create a safe space in which your partner can tell you the truth. No one likes to be castigated. Creating a space for truth telling doesn't mean that you can't feel sad, agitated, or angry with your partner. It does mean that you need to practice sidestepping the knee-jerk reactions you're tempted to make when your partner summons the courage to 'fess up. Try saying something like, "This really upsets me, but I'm glad you told me." Once your partner sees how your reactions open the way to honesty—and once he realizes how good honesty feels—he may begin to allow you the space to do the same. That's a plus, because the best way to encourage truth telling is to do it yourself.

Make a habit of coming clean with each other.
You will squirm sometimes. But the payoff in
trust is huge, and worth pursuing.

What It Takes

"The giving of love is an education in itself."
Eleanor Roosevelt

Marriage invites us to make generosity a daily practice. It asks us to move over, emotionally and physically, to let another in. This doesn't feel comfortable. While we welcome the closeness our partner brings, we resist the inroads he makes on our emotions. Yet there can be no true intimacy without this deeper exposure. It's like sex the first time with anyone: One reason it's intimate is that you are naked in front of another person whose caring and approval matter desperately to you. Marriage requires you to get naked emotionally with your partner. You will feel very exposed. But there can be no deepening of the closeness between you without this gradual peeling-away of your defenses. Dive into your generosity—give those layers up—and open yourself to the new territory to be explored.

◌◌

Marriage opens you up very wide. It requires a bright courage.
It asks you to give and give again. It is natural to struggle against it
at times, for this is nothing less than a test of the spirit.

You're Weird

*"The reality of the other person is not in what he reveals
to you, but in what he cannot reveal to you."*

Kahlil Gibran, *Sand and Foam*

I t wasn't so bad, walking to work through the snow," I told my husband on the phone one morning. "I went over to Park Avenue, where I figured the doormen would shovel the sidewalks in front of their fancy apartment buildings."

"Wow," my husband said, "that sounds incredibly sensible."

It's not that my husband thinks I'm an idiot. But I realized in that moment how stressful it was for him to live with my way of intuitively sensing things. It takes courage and faith for him to comprehend my way of thinking.

We are all aliens to each other but so familiar to ourselves that our oddities escape us. Every day you are doing and saying things that your partner may be at a loss to comprehend. That he tries to understand is a testament to his great spirit. That he gives up trying and simply accepts is nothing short of a miracle.

*You are an alien on your partner's planet.
Respect the gift of his tolerance.*

The Tyranny of Perfection

"Nothing endures but change."

Heraclitus, from Diogenes Laertius, *Lives of Eminent Philosophers*

We live in a culture that constantly sets standards for achievement. All our lives we accept these evaluations of where we stand in the form of grades, test scores, and performance reviews. Marriage has no such landmarks. There is no way to chart progress or know if we're doing well at it. Anniversaries measure only the surface length of marriage, not its depth—and in marriage, depth is everything.

Marriage takes a long time and is always a work in progress. It can't ever be finished, even if one of you dies. It continues to work on you, shaping who you become in the world. A process so broad, so powerful, cannot be measured by any terms we know. You are never "there" or "finished." Don't expect to "get it right," either. Doing marriage right is not the goal. Keeping it deeply alive is.

*Marriage can't be graded like a test. It will not serve up
its riches in a framework of right and wrong. Instead, look for
periods of deep turbulence framed by stretches of deep
contentment. That is the measure of marriage.*

A Friendly Push

"The best way is to come uphill with me / And have our fire and laugh and be afraid."
Robert Frost, "The Bonfire"

In a working marriage, each partner pushes the other to go the extra mile. It's not really about pushing, however, so much as it is about being like athletes in a relay, passing the baton so one surges forward when the other is temporarily spent. My husband cajoles me into going to the museum one freezing Saturday night, when I would have stayed indoors swaddled in lethargy. I cajole him into inviting friends over or making a special meal rather than taking the easy way out with the same old, same old. In this way we pull each other forward, hand over hand, with our unique energies and talents. When one of us gets tired, the other's drive carries us both; when the other hangs back, the first is revived and takes up the cause.

Notice how your individual energies come
into play in your marriage. See how they mingle
and dance, impel and ignite.

One Plus One Equals One

"All they could see was sky, water, birds, light, and confluence.
It was the whole morning world."
Eudora Welty, *The Optimist's Daughter*

It is our first Christmas alone together. We waken entwined against the frigid weather outside. The cat sits, purring, on our chests. We are a family: two lumps and a little lump, huddled and happy in the safe world we have made. We are joined; we are "we." When did this happen?

Watch for signs of the family you are becoming. They will come upon you as quietly as a cat creeping for comfort; will burst upon you like cold winter air. They will make you calm and reverent. They will take your breath away.

Revere the union you have created.

Comforting Yourself

"The spirits that I summoned up / I now can't rid myself of."
Johann Wolfgang von Goethe, "The Sorcerer's Apprentice"

Emotions are unruly. There is no point trying to talk yourself out of them. When you're caught in a volatile conflict with your spouse, or when you are wrestling in silence with something you can't (or won't) express to him, don't waste energy trying to talk yourself out of your feelings. Instead, ask your feelings, "What do you want? What are you trying to tell me? I'm listening." Let them rage, scream, sob at you. Calmly hear them out. Tell them, "I'm smart and I'm strong. I'll take care of you." Then take a deep breath and approach the situation, free of their grip but filled with their truth, able to use your mind to resolve the turmoil in your soul.

❧

Talk to your emotions rather than setting them loose on your partner.
Tell them they're in good hands and will be handled in good time.

Coverups

"When you have faults, do not fear to abandon them."

Simonides 1:8

My husband and I have a friend who is simple and loving, unburdened by intellect, and free of pretense. He is happy and clear, abundant in energy, generous to a fault. His lesson to us is that when the space taken up by pretension is freed, there is an openness, a clarity, that shines through.

Don't apply your mind to pretense with your partner. A better use of your energy is to seek to understand the honest core of yourself and to look for ways to express this more freely and clearly to him. Pretense is a power trip—an abuse of others' loving trust. Practicing it on your partner is a disrespectful act.

Beneath your need to save face and be right
lies your true self—the self your partner fell in love
with and wants to see; the self that binds you to
others because it is the self we all share.

Tread Softly

"The greatest fault of a penetrating wit is to go beyond the mark."
François, Duc de la Rochefoucauld, *Reflections*

Sometimes you're going to run headlong into your partner's pain. You won't realize you've done it until he reacts—perhaps with a flash of anger designed to put you off the scent, or with silence. When his response seems inappropriate or out of proportion to the situation, you are probably confronting very old fears and beliefs, often learned in childhood, always learned the hard way. Use these as clues: They are valuable opportunities, not as weapons to win an argument, but to see more deeply into your partner.

*Volatility is a sign that you are touching a
nerve in your partner, viewing a place that few
people ever see. Rather than press your advantage,
tread respectfully and let change unfold slowly,
as your partner can tolerate it.*

Growth

"The shapes a bright container can contain!"
Theodore Roethke, "I Knew a Woman"

When your husband is not around for a period of time—perhaps he is traveling or has been called away from you—you may feel your inner self begin to unfold, expand, and flower. Maybe you visit friends, go out solo to movies or shops, revert to slovenly bachelor housekeeping, and revel in having the television, the bathroom, and the ice cream all to yourself. It's natural to enjoy this autonomy. We need to feel in control of our world as much as we need to feel bonded to others—and marriage, there's no doubt, challenges our sense of control. So enjoy your bachelor time.

There may be cause for concern, however, if you feel angry or depressed upon your partner's return. Some readjustment is always needed, but if your emotions are all in the negative, you may need to investigate why your husband's absence has come to mean freedom for you.

❧

*Freedom should be cultivated within your marriage,
not illicitly enjoyed outside it. Your partner has no right to
limit your horizons, but it is not his task to broaden
them, either. That is your responsibility.*

Experimentation

"It hurteth not the tongue to give fair words."
John Heywood, *Proverbs*

Learn to keep out of the way. Many women have been trained from the cradle to perform many tasks at once and to do all of them "just right." When your partner tries a task familiar to you but new to him, don't interfere with the execution or criticize the results. Students learn best when they bump into obstacles, figure out puzzles, and find their own way through the maze.

Make yourself available for questions, but don't hang over your partner. Let him feel he can come to you for help and that he'll receive it free of criticism. Let him make his own inroads on the task and enjoy a sense of accomplishment. Then he will begin to claim ownership of the endeavor—and you won't be stuck doing it alone anymore.

∾

Create a relaxed atmosphere for learning new skills.

Self-Sacrifice

"It is idle to play the lyre for an ass."
Saint Jerome

D o you do things "for the relationship" rather than because *you* want to? That can lead to conflict if your good intentions aren't met with the appreciation you think they deserve. Your anger then becomes an accusation: "I did it for you!" Your mate will sense the injustice of this and naturally will defend himself.

A variant of this problem occurs when a couple vows to give up habits together: to stop smoking, eat less, exercise more, and so on. It's a good idea in principle, but what happens if he backslides and you don't? Will you be angry at him because he didn't persevere, while you did? If so, you'll need to ask yourself why you undertook the activity in the first place. Perhaps your anger and sense of betrayal spring from the fact that you did it more for his sake than for yours.

∽

When you make a decision, ask yourself whether you would feel glad you made it even if your spouse didn't hold up his end of the bargain. That way you do not lose yourself in the marriage.

Open to Desire

"A shudder of joy runs up / The trunk: the needles tingle; / One bird uncontrollably cries,/ The wind changes round, and I stir / Within another's life. Whose life?"

James Dickey, "In the Tree House at Night"

Y ou have to be sexually open," a friend observes about marital sex, "willing to be drawn into your partner's desire." Sometimes nothing kindles. Fatigue or anger may be the culprit. The former is transient; the latter needs talking about. Sometimes we simply need to be brought back to our sexual selves, reacquainted with that part of us that keeps us happy, whole, well defended against the fragmentation of daily life. Through sexual expression, we let our partner help us to find ourselves again.

Receive sexual advances in the spirit of free experimentation. They need not always "lead" anywhere. But where they do lead may surprise you.

Table It

"The storm had rolled away to faintness like a wagon crossing a bridge."
Eudora Welty, *A Curtain of Green*, *"A Piece of News"*

There are times in marriage when we just can't face a confrontation. Too much other bad stuff has happened that day; or we are feeling stripped of all our diplomatic powers; or we are feeling too fragile for criticism. It's OK in such cases to say, "I can't talk about this now. I'm too angry/hurt/distracted. Let's talk after dinner/after I get back from my run/tomorrow morning." You have an obligation to hear about problems, but you have the right to hear them on your own terms. If the timing is off, it's best to admit that you can't listen very well right now, but that you'd like to talk at a later time. If you use this as an avoidance strategy, your partner will rightly sense it and call you on it. But if you are judicious and honest in your response, your partner may honor your needs because he sees that you really want to resolve the problem, not just argue about it.

Not all conflicts must be handled as soon as they arise.
Find the time and place that work best for both of you.

Being a Sport

"There is, however, a limit at which forbearance ceases to be a virtue."
Edmund Burke, *Observations on a Late Publication on the Present State of the Nation*

Y ou're a good sport," my husband tells me. Debatable, I think, fuming over his latest transgression. I probably am a good sport, but I used to think that meant I wasn't allowed to get unreasonably angry—or be unreasonable—about things that mattered to me. Now I know that being a good sport does not equal being a pushover. It means playing the game of marriage with aplomb, giving in on some points with good grace in exchange for the ones your partner allows. It means knowing when to back off from your position, letting your partner do things his way. It *doesn't* mean you can never take up that position again or drive aggressively to make your points or win a goal.

Being a good sport is a voluntary, occasional relinquishment of power. If either adjective doesn't describe what's happening, then you are not participating in the marriage as an equal.

Criticism

> *"He who would distinguish true from false must have
> an adequate idea of what is true and false."*
>
> Benedict Spinoza, *Ethics*

I hate being criticized. And I hear just about everything as criticism. My fat old ego gets in the way, deflecting a well-meant truth. "How come you think everything is a slight?" my husband snaps. It's a hard habit to break, this endless self-defense. It's harder still to listen not just with an open mind but also with an open heart. It takes a lot of trust to consider that maybe our partner's harsh words are coming from an honest, loving place; to give our partner's motives the benefit of the doubt.

∽

*Before you kick sand in your partner's face,
look for a grain of truth.*

Exposed

"And they were both naked, the man and his wife, and were not ashamed."

Genesis 2:24–25

My husband knows me so well, I don't know whether to be grateful or enraged. He blows my cover when I try to save face in an argument. He won't rise to the bait when I'm itching for a fight.

It's unnerving to have someone know us so well that none of our usual tricks work. It feels as if we have been caught naked. But as clearly as our partner can see our manipulations, so he can see our pain also and embrace it without even having to understand it. When my husband takes one look at me and folds me in his arms, I'm glad that, to him, I am as transparent as glass.

∽

You can't be understood as you've always longed to be without being revealed as never before.

Thrills and Chills

"Most folks are about as happy as they make up their minds to be."
Abraham Lincoln

Sex—how much, how little, how often? Here's a true thing about sex: it's never the same, and it's never only good or only bad. Sometimes it's hotter than other times. Sometimes you're having sex a lot; sometimes not much. The only time any of that is a problem is if one of you thinks it is. The only way to know this is (you guessed it) to talk about it. When things are great, tell each other how great things are. When fatigue, hectic schedules, or crossed wires are the order of the day, tell each other that you miss one another, so both of you know that you haven't lost interest or, worse, forgotten the forgettable!

Make time to rekindle. But when you have no time,
have faith that the spark is there.

Having to Win

"'I'm demonstrating the misuse of free speech. To prove that it exists.'"
Rosencrantz, in *Rosencrantz and Guildenstern Are Dead,* by Tom Stoppard

I love to have the last word. So does my husband. This compulsion can keep the tiff going for hours, punctuated by long, fuming silences while we each marshal ammunition for the next salvo. Since neither of us is feeling listened to, we continue to vie for the upper hand in the sparring. Often this last-word business becomes a battle of escalating insults, each person outdoing the other, until some exceptionally dirty old rag of history is dragged out and flung in the opponent's face. Then cold silence descends.

Eventually one of us has to let go of the need to be right. That is the only way to open up space for the other person to concede that our point of view might—just *might*—have some merit. That is the only way to shift the dialogue from self-justification toward solution.

⟨✿⟩

Having the last word doesn't necessarily mean that you have been heard. If your arguments take you around in circles, try removing the ego from your conversation and see how the dialogue changes.

Whom Are You Protecting?

"We are, perhaps, uniquely among the earth's creatures, the worrying animal."
Lewis Thomas, *The Medusa and the Snail*, "The Youngest and Brightest Thing Around"

It's frightening for us when the people we love court danger. My husband rides his bicycle all over Manhattan in blinding snowstorms and screaming rush-hour traffic. He's been tossed atop taxis, drenched in puddles, and sideswiped by sadistic drivers. He wears a helmet and he's a careful, confident rider, but I'm haunted by visions of crushed head or crippled hands. Should my fears make him stop? I don't think so. He is not, after all, doing anything irresponsible or spiteful. He's just doing his thing. We don't have the right to demand that people we love be less than fully who they are simply because their exuberant selves make us worried, frightened, or uncomfortable. We must let them be in the world, blessing them for who they are, not for who we'd like them to be.

❧

It's not our partner's job to make us feel comfortable and safe,
confident and cared for. Serenity is our responsibility.

Growth Feels Dangerous

*"The easy, gentle, and sloping path . . . is not the path of true virtue.
It demands a rough and thorny road."*

Michel Eyquem de Montaigne, *Essays*

Our body will do anything to maintain the status quo. Just when we try hardest to lose weight, for example, our body worries that it might starve, and it slows our metabolism so we stay at the same old hated poundage. We perspire or goose-pimple as our body works to keep its temperature at the 98.6° norm.

This drive for sameness is called homeostasis. If our body strives for the status quo, can our nature be any different? The trouble is, emotional homeostasis can stunt our growth. When marriage challenges us to feel more deeply, to reach down and find new strength, skill, and understanding, we resist with all we've got—because we're being asked to leave the stable shores we know so well. In every molecule, we experience this as danger.

*A profound sense of danger is a clue that a path for
growth has been opened in your marriage. Rather than
resist, persist. Sit with the danger until it becomes familiar.
Then go a little deeper and sit again. And so on.*

Your Space

"I had three chairs in my house: one for solitude,
two for friendship, three for society."

Henry David Thoreau, *Walden*

Carve out some space in your home that is yours alone. Present this to your partner not as if it were negotiable but simply as a puzzle that you and he must solve: "If we put the bureau here, where am I going to have my desk/office/studio/reading chair?" Both of you deserve a space of your own, where there is no trace of others' presence. Don't give in to the temptation to merge everything, just because your lives are now being spent together. Even in the smallest living space, a tabletop, a chair, several drawers, and a lamp can be designated as one person's turf. You will discover that finding the space is not nearly so hard as claiming it for your own.

❧

Being one with your partner does not extend to
letting him take over the environment so no trace of
"you" remains. State your boundaries with grace
and clarity, as many times as it takes.

Your Handiwork

"Understanding is joyous."
Carl Sagan, *Broca's Brain*

Working late one night, I called home: "How about Chinese take-out?" My husband laughed. "Funny you should ask. On the way home, I picked up a menu from that new restaurant up the street." Remember to relish your evolving partnership: the wonderful symmetries between you; the easy way you toss the ball of life back and forth. You may be struggling with many areas of stress, but remember that there once was a time when you didn't even know each other's middle names. Look at how far you have come in your understanding of one another.

Admire the process of partnership as it unfolds naturally between you, the result of your dedication and steadfast love.

Small Stuff/Big Stuff

"The boy called, 'Wolf, wolf!' and the villagers came out to help him."
Aesop, *The Shepherd Boy and the Wolf*

Some conflicts must be worked out; some must be waited out; a few are serious enough that they must be handled immediately, at all costs. If you treat every crisis at the same level of magnitude, your partner will stop listening when you need him to listen the most. Who can attend, consider, and resolve with equal skill all the time? Since you are honored to have someone whose desire is to listen to you and love you, learn how to weigh problems and attend to the biggest ones first. Once the biggies are taken care of, many smaller issues may recede in importance.

One large conflagration over the right issue clears the air
better than a dozen skirmishes around the perimeter.

Hot Spots

"The will to do, the soul to dare."
Sir Walter Scott, "The Lady of the Lake"

Every marriage has "hot spots" that neither partner wants to touch. They are usually subjects that cause deep flareups between you. The "hot spots" list begins to be compiled very early in courtship, when both of you start to realize the importance of the relationship, and the instinct to preserve the bond exerts its power. Sometimes these spots are so hot that we won't even admit them to ourselves, much less thrash them out with our partner.

Take some time to notice where these hot spots appear in your marriage. Practice articulating them to yourself. When you forge into one, stand there quietly and take in the landscape from that vantage point. What does the relationship look like from there? What's so terrifying about being there? What feelings are triggered by just the thought of that hot spot?

Step slowly into forbidden terrain. You will survive
the experience. Venturing out is a brave thing.

Discomfort

....

"Be not afraid of sudden fear."
Proverbs 3:25

We all have comfort zones that define how much we risk each day of our lives. We have a comfort zone for how hard we exercise, how hard we work, how much we tell people about ourselves. This doesn't mean that we don't feel discomfort; we do. But our levels of discomfort are comfortable to us.

You know you are about to step outside of your comfort zone with your partner when you feel absolutely certain, for all kinds of very logical reasons, that what you're contemplating simply cannot happen without disastrous consequences. When this kind of discomfort arises in your marriage, you're being offered a golden opportunity to move to a new level of closeness with your partner. To claim that prize, try to push your tolerance for standing in your discomfort zone just a bit further each time you find yourself there.

∽

Discomfort is a sign of growth. Be encouraged
that you have become strong enough to stand in that space.

A New Focus

"And the combat ceased for want of combatants."
Pierre Corneille, *Le Cid*

Think about something your partner does that infuriates you. You probably have found that trying to change him in this regard only antagonizes him. Try focusing on his *behavior* instead of on him. Ask yourself what it would take to change the behavior. Then act in a way that is consistent with the change you seek.

When you shift your attention in this way, your language and actions will move away from attacking your partner, toward solving the problem. Anger at your partner no longer rules you. Your partner may have been resisting you because he felt the personal accusations behind your words. Your change in focus frees him to do the same. Now he can notice what the behavior is doing to your relationship, not how you are hurting him.

〰️

Instead of focusing on the problem, focus on the results you seek.
Notice how this changes your interactions with your partner.

Anything Goes

My husband washes the dishes naked!" my friend says, laughing. So does mine. I wish more women had been brought up to have that kind of comfort with their bodies. Nothing about bodies makes my husband squeamish. Any sound, sight, or function is OK by him, and he does them all with enjoyment. The freedom he feels relaxes us both. No appearances need be kept up. I realize now the effort it takes to create the illusion of superhumanity. It's much nicer to loll nude on the couch, watching trashy television, pinching each other at the funny parts. It's much nicer to get naked with someone who loves us.

◦◦

Forget veneers and varnishes. Let your marriage be a place where anything can happen.

Participation

"'Love should be put into action!' / screamed the old hermit. /
Across the pond an echo / tried and tried to confirm it."
Elizabeth Bishop, "Chemin de Fer"

I don't take for granted the fact that we're married," a woman told me. "He can leave anytime." Our partner is not like an old lamp or shoe—we don't know all his angles. We can't assume he'll stay in our life as long as we want him. What happens if he decides *he* doesn't want *us*?

Marriage is not a right conferred upon us. We must keep ourselves worthy of it. If we are bored, it's our responsibility to do something about it, not passively to keep score of every flaw.

◦◦◦

In marriage, you either stay or go.
There is no place here for one who sits and waits.

Leave Him Alone

"The truly silent, who keep apart, / He is like a tree grown in a meadow."
Amenemope, *The Instruction of Amenemope*

L et your partner have his sadness and anger. He cannot be an open book to you. There will be many times when he needs to be inaccessible, quiet and alone. It's his prerogative to draw into himself; all of us need to take refuge from time to time. This is the place where we must go to struggle, to renew, to resolve. When your partner is doing this, don't interfere with his process. He will share when he's ready.

∞

When your partner pulls away from you, watch quietly and stay available. Let him trust you with himself in his own time.

Where Change Is Born

"Spur not an unbroken horse, put not your plowshare too deep into new land."
Sir Walter Scott, *The Monastery*

Clothes on the floor. Apple cores on the bookshelf. Lateness. Forgetfulness. You fill in the blank with the behaviors that drive you crazy. Yelling will only ensure that you'll have to yell frequently. Doing tasks for him will only reinforce the idea that he needn't bother. Calmly explaining your point of view may help him comprehend you on a rational level, but your point of view doesn't belong to him; merely hearing it won't give rise to change.

Before we can change, we must see a benefit to it that we can relate to and value. Then change becomes a logical extension of ourselves, not something imposed upon us. When the benefit of picking up his clothes makes sense to him, your partner's behavior will change accordingly. The benefit could be many things: it could be that you'll be nicer to be around . . . that his clothes won't be inadvertently stepped on by you in whatever dirty shoes you happen to be wearing . . . that his favorite shirt is clean and ready to be worn because it was tossed into the laundry, not under the bed.

Intrinsically motivated change takes time, but it lasts longer.
Stay patient and live your life straight ahead,
with consequences coming as they come.

A Different Kindling

"I found my lover on his bed, and my heart was sweet to excess."
Love Songs of the New Kingdom

Remember when love between you was new, and when your lover entered a crowded room, you felt a jolt of excitement; an electric awareness of every move he made? Where does that little spark go after long familiarity?

Paradoxically, time—the very thing that increases your intimacy—evaporates this intensity. The old spark once kept aglow by mystery now must be kindled by reverence for your deep knowledge of each other. Who else has tended you when you were ill, cuddled you through terrors, stuck with you through furies, and helped you survive disasters? Your intimacy now may not have the sharp, sweet edge of that early excitement. But its steady glow illuminates, while passion only ignites.

Why chase the spark when you have made fire?

A Danger Sign

"'I do desire we may be better strangers.'"

Orlando, in *As You Like It*, by William Shakespeare

If passion is marriage's fuel, apathy is its poison. Even when passion is expressed in arguments, it's important to care enough to fight!

When you give up fighting for your vision of your marriage, red flags should go up. Sound the alarm to your partner before you feel apathy's deadly hand. Knowing that you both still care can pull you together on an island of common ground, however small, in the sea of differences between you.

Stay in touch with your desire to make your marriage work.
Don't confuse resignation with acceptance.

Contentment As a State of Mind

"Weary not thyself to seek for more."
Amenemope, *The Instruction of Amenemope*

The practice of contentment can occur even when you are not contented. That doesn't mean faking happiness. It does mean choosing sometimes to adopt a discipline of silence so your partnership can move forward and find new territory rather than go over and over the same old paths. What is the benefit of having the same argument sixty times, after all? Your partner knows very well what is bothering you. State your position once more, calmly and completely. Then rest within yourself, trusting the unseen process of change.

∽

Sometimes you can't get there any faster than you're already going.
Don't let your longing for the destination keep you
from quiet enjoyment of the journey.

Begin Again

"I take off my hat, unpainted / and figurative, to you. / Again I promise to try."
Elizabeth Bishop, "Manuelzinho"

Coming off a weekend filled with spats, tiffs, and tears, we tread softly around each other Monday morning. There is a healing that happens during the night that has made us forget what the fights were about, leaving only shadows of exhaustion and a wish to start over. I've come to count on this feeling as a way to rout out the habit of picking up the argument midstream, hanging onto the threads of rage all through the night. Basically it's easier to connect than to fight. When the content of the fight degenerates into the blinding desire to make one's point, the point itself becomes irrelevant. So this morning, I cover up his shoulders with the sheet, warming him, before I get up to write. He mumbles and rubs his toes against mine. We start a new day.

*Pay attention to your urge to reconnect rather
than continue the turbulence. Sometimes it's better
to move on than to make your point.*

Coming Attractions

"As an apple tree among the trees of the wood, so is my beloved among young men."
The Song of Solomon 2:3

Don't expect to stop looking at other men just because you're married. Don't expect your husband to stop looking at other women, either. The opposite sex is always interesting, in all its numbers, shapes, and forms. Looking is no betrayal of your spouse; it's an expression of yourself as a curious, sexual being. Fantasy is free and blameless. Using fantasy habitually to withdraw from your partner emotionally or sexually, however, is not. It's a sign that something has come between you that needs to be worked out. The object of the attraction is only a symbol of that intervention. Don't waste time fighting about that. Root out the deeper problem and you'll be getting closer to the truths that need expression.

⁐⁐

Interest in others is not the problem.
Lack of interest in each other is.

Why You Fell in Love

"I both love and do not love, and am mad and am not mad."
Anacreon, *Fragment 79*

One evening, harried and in a hurry to put dinner on the table, I ordered my husband, "Do something with those potatoes!" He started to juggle them. Not exactly what I had in mind, but effective at getting me to laugh and let go of my bad day.

My husband's screwball spontaneity, his disarming wit, and his exuberance are what make him eternally interesting. These same qualities also contribute to his infallible talent for losing phone numbers within minutes of jotting them down; his penchant for leaving the ice cream container open on the kitchen table while he dashes into the living room to catch something on TV; his reliably stubborn way of not fitting into my perfectly planned life. If I nag him about these things, however, I chip away at the very traits that attracted me to him in the first place. I may get what I want—an orderly, deliberate husband—but I also get what I don't want: a partner who is ordinary and predictable, and very unhappy.

❧

*You fell in love with your husband because of the person
he is. Seek the essence of his character beneath all his other
shenanigans. It'll help you shrug off the small stuff.*

Drama

"A sharp tongue is the only edged tool that grows keener with constant use."
Washington Irving, *Rip van Winkle*

I am sometimes an in-the-flesh, in-your-face bitch. I hear myself saying things that make my hair stand on end. My husband takes my tirades in good stride, sometimes just listening, sometimes cajoling me out of my mood, sometimes giving me a verbal cuff or two in return.

We must guard against too often turning the tool of language into a weapon against someone we love. Certainly there are times when our mate needs a talking-to. All I urge here is moderation—and taking a moment to think before letting loose. Are we legitimately furious about the matter at hand, or are we lashing out about some hidden insult or hurt? Is there another way to handle the situation?

We cannot expect our partner to repair his wrongs if we wrong him.

It's easier to be nasty than it is to be clear.
Practice right action over acting out.

Good-bye, Hello

*"A lively understandable spirit / Once entertained you. /
It will come again. / Be still. / Wait."*
Theodore Roethke, The Lost Son, 5. "It Was Beginning Winter"

Working hard on separate projects, my husband and I haven't seen much of each other over the past few days. Yet when we finally get together, the first thing that happens is a tiff about some stupid thing. This seems to be a fact of how we relate: We reunite; we fight—when all we want to do is enjoy each other.

Perhaps this happens as a way to stake out territory within the marriage once again. Perhaps we are working off the tension of two coming together as one after operating solo all week, with no one to please but ourselves. Perhaps we're disappointed to find that, even though they're the person we've longed to see, they still have all the warts that drive us crazy.

The only thing that helps in such situations is to remember that we didn't intend "hello" to be this way, and to start over, with feeling.

*Separations confer anxiety, exhilaration, loneliness, freedom.
It's natural for things to be rocky for a while afterward.
Stay with it. It doesn't mean anything.*

Healing Sleep

"There is a time for many words, and there is also a time for sleep."
Homer, *The Odyssey*

When my husband and I wake up in the morning, before either of us stirs, I notice we are breathing together, deep and long, in perfect rhythm. It seems to me that the night has wrought a small miracle of reattunement. Perhaps in the unconscious hours we spend sleeping, there is a repairing of the tears, scars, rifts, and divisions that the day creates. In just the way that wounds heal and tired muscles renew themselves in the night, perhaps sleeping together reknits our spirits.

Go to sleep touching each other.
Partake of the healing of the night.

Drama, Scenes, Acts, and Plays

"What manner of speech has escaped the barrier of your teeth?"
Homer, *The Iliad*

Sometimes we hold things in until we're furious. Then we make a scene. We may get the results we want, but we usually get them in an atmosphere of resentment. Then no one has won.

I tend to assume that without drama, I won't be listened to. Of course, there's no guarantee that stating my wishes clearly and calmly will get me my way. For me, practicing moderation is not about getting what I want. Rather, it's a discipline in maintaining the steady conviction that I deserve to be heard; that I don't have to yell to make my points worth hearing. Even if I don't get the results I want, I have the satisfaction of knowing that I handled myself as I wanted to, not as I was compelled to.

∽

Don't make scenes. Your voice will
be heard better without them.

Stop Talking

"- - - - - - - - - - - - -"

Harpo Marx

Find a nonverbal way to communicate. Words aren't the only route to reconciliation. Touch came before talk in our earliest life, and words can get us into trouble. There are times, after an argument, when we are still hurting and wanting to make our point, but we also are missing the comradeship of the other person. If we talk about things, however, the hot spots will flare up and we'll be arguing again. At times like these, nonverbal connection can lead us out of the maze. It needn't be affectionate—at our house we stick our tongues out at each other ("You hurt me and I'm still mad, but I am ready to acknowledge your existence by sticking my tongue out at you.") It's juvenile, but then, so are many of our arguments. If we can admit this, we can reestablish contact and go forward together. Later we will feel calm enough to talk things out from a place of unity, not angry isolation.

Reconnect with your hearts before you connect with words.
Then, rebonded, apply your minds to the situation.

Attachment

It's unnerving to notice how bonded I already am to my husband. When he's working hard and spending two or three nights a week in his studio, I get sad and even weepy, suffering the lack of his attention. I used to be ashamed of this: Here I was, a strong and independent woman with plenty of things to do in her spare time, craving her husband's attention. Now I've decided it would be odd *not* to miss what I've spent thousands of hours nurturing. We're good together. We make each other happy. We calm each other down and stir each other up. We've labored for that deep knowledge of one another; worked hard to find and keep that edge of passion and solace. When I don't have it, I want it, and that's good and natural.

*Reaping the comfort of your hard
work is half the fun of marriage.*

Courage

"My valor is certainly going!—it is sneaking off! I feel
it oozing out, as it were, at the palm of my hands!"
Richard Brinsley Sheridan, *The Rivals*

It's tiring to stick to your guns. Backing off to a safe haven looks tempting when facing the blast of our partner's anger. But if you entered the fray for an important reason—your freedom or dignity or the good of the marriage—grab your courage in both hands and hang on. Your partner may be resisting strongly because you have touched a nerve of truth. He's fighting that truth, not you. He's raging at the messenger because the message itself is unassailable. Make your case; let him be alone to think about it; reconnect later to see what has transpired. Meantime, do the self-nurturing things you need to do in order to keep your resolve strong.

❧

When you would like to quit, persist and observe
what happens when you see something through to its very end.

Let Yourself Be Cared For

"She brought forth butter in a lordly dish."
Joshua 5:25

I'm sitting in my husband's art studio, eating the breakfast he has prepared of instant coffee and gingersnaps. We spent last night here, and this morning he's taking very good care of me, calibrating the temperature of my shower, letting me sleep twelve hours without interruption. Allowing your partner to take care of you is as much an act of generosity on your part as it is on his. It's important to make him feel indispensable to the fulfillment of your desires. People want to feel that they make a difference. Allowing your partner to act on his natural, noble desire to care for you is one small, simple way to do that.

*When your partner wants to care for you, he is
giving you the gift of his best self. Sink into it. We're
lucky to have this very direct way to express
our goodness to each other.*

Resolution

"Only when the year grows cold do we see that the pine and cypress are the last to fade."

Confucius, *Analects of Confucius*

Does it seem as though your problems are becoming more and more difficult the longer you are married? Perhaps this is because you are grappling with issues that are more serious, more deeply attached to your essential characters. You are pushing on each other's boundaries, demanding deeper entrance to one another's lives. Perhaps you despair because the problems seem bigger, tougher, more convoluted, more intractable. Perhaps you wonder if you and your partner are losing your ability to communicate or compromise. But in fact you are growing to a new level of comfort with each other, one where you are able to wrestle longer and harder because you trust each other to persevere until an outcome is reached—or even if it is never reached.

It's a good sign when the problems get harder. It means you both feel safe enough to rock the boat—and skilled and strong enough to keep rowing even when there's no shore in sight.

Free to Go

"All day I climb myself / Bowlegged up those damned poles
rooster-heeled in all / Kinds of weather."
James Dickey, "Power and Light"

Not a day goes by that you couldn't find a good reason to get divorced," my mother once told me. She and my father have been married for fifty years. After fifty years, are the "good reasons" still the same? It would be boring to have the same reasons; disheartening to have new ones. Yet I take comfort in her words, which promise me that a marriage can remain alive, full of static and connection, and that thoughts of jumping overboard are unnatural only in their *absence*. What a relief! Now I can fantasize mutiny without fear that thinking equals doing. Marriage becomes a choice, freely chosen, each day.

∽

Knowing you can leave gives you the choice to stay.
The open door is a sign of your commitment to remain.

Niceties

"Ritual, ritual! Does it mean no more than presents of jade and silk?"

Confucius, *Analects of Confucius*

This has been said before, but it bears repeating: Don't forget to say please and thank you. Just because the two of you are now stuck together for life (and you aren't, don't forget) doesn't mean you mutate into beings who don't long to be acknowledged for the accumulated little "goods" you do each day in the world. Sometimes, when you're in one of those impasses where not much else can be discussed level-headedly, niceties are your neutral territory. Use them until you can cross safely into the enemy's camp with other, more heartfelt, phrases, like "I'm sorry."

❧

Don't underestimate the power of courtesy to soften battlelines.
When honestly expressed and consciously practiced, courtesy is
a manifestation of your deep respect for your partner.

Your Family and Friends

"I have often regretted my speech, never my silence."
Publilius Syrus, Maxim 1070

Let your husband find his own way of relating to your family and friends. It's tempting to want to intervene, interlocute, make them like each other. This has much more to do with our need to integrate all the spheres of our life than it does with helping our husband. Introduce them, provide some backdrop of common ground—perhaps a topic you know interests them both—and let them find their own footing. They've made the wary small talk of new acquaintances many times before. And they know what's at stake here. If they want to come together out of love for you, they will do so. If not, your prodding, wishing, or pushing won't help.

*Don't organize your husband's experience of your
friends and family members. They are grownups.
As you love them, so you must trust them.*

His Family and Friends

"Without any intentional, fancy way of adjusting yourself,
to express yourself as you are is the most important thing."
Shunryu Suzuki, *Zen Mind, Beginner's Mind*

Sometimes it's difficult to establish a genuine way of connecting with our spouse's family or friends. It's hard to forge a unique connection, as we would normally do in friendship, because we are drawn into the role through our husbands. If you are inclined, establish contact directly: Create your own unique relationship, outside the one with your spouse. Call to chat; send a gift from you alone. Show the fullness of who you are so you can be judged on your own merits, not on what you represent or symbolize when occupying the role of wife, stepmother, or daughter-in-law.

୧୦

Don't let your spouse be the filter through
which you experience others. Let people meet
and see you on your terms.

Role Rules

"For as long as she could remember, Mrs. Bridge had known that unless she was wearing slacks—slacks were worn only for gardening—she must wear stockings."

Evan S. Connell, *Mrs. Bridge*

It's easy to talk a good game about role reversal—until it happens to us. Did you ever think you might be the one paying all the bills or doing the taxes or working late while your spouse waits at home? Could you have suspected that he'd be better with babies than you are? It's unnerving to experience marriage from what has traditionally been the "other's" point of view. It's also unnerving to run full tilt into all our sneaky expectations about what we are "supposed" to do in marriage.

With freedom from the constraints of old roles comes the responsibility to shape new ones to fit our needs. There is a burden on each partner to speak up about what each expects from the other. These conversations can be painful, as they touch the deepest nerves about what men and women want from each other and from marriage. They beg to be avoided. If you do that, however, the decisions will be made anyway, willy-nilly, and you may be left with constant low-level anger. Is that the trade-off you really want?

❧

Confront the role issue. Take it on with persistence and tact.
Keep fine-tuning your roles until they fit each of you better.
Perfect fits are an illusion, but you need to have a role
that you like getting up to play each day.

Share the Attraction

"We danced, / in our minds, / and read a book together. / You remember?"
William Carlos Williams, "Asphodel, That Greeny Flower"

Take time to tell each other what you saw in one another when you first met. What was it about your husband that intrigued and attracted you? Perhaps his crooked smile? The slight old-man stoop of his shoulders? The way he said please and thank you to the waiter? His diffidence? His confidence? It's nice to know what our partner saw in us—it connects us to a time when the energy between us was thunderous, crackling with possibility.

❧

Together, remember your common history.
Sharing it with each other binds you together.

Creating Your Future

"If thou follow thy star, thou canst not fail of a glorious haven."
Dante Alighieri, *The Divine Comedy,* Canto xv

reams for the future can be hard to reconcile with the reality of the present. How do we get from here to there? we wonder. Dreams help a lifetime partnership flower—otherwise how could we persevere through the difficult patches? But when what we want seems so distant from what we have, the dissonance can feel unbearable. Some couples benefit from drawing up a plan; some by feeling their way through the organic process of living and changing. Or you may want to plan, while your partner wants to "flow"—or vice versa. A common ground to start from is the "now" you share and the fact that the two of you is all you have when more transient trappings fall away. Work from this union, with your future union in mind.

In planning your future, whatever keeps you intact,
individually and together, is worth investigating.

Proceed with Caution

"One never goes so far as when one doesn't know where one is going."
Johann Wolfgang von Goethe, *Letter to Karl Friedrich Zelter*

I warn him, 'Stop, before there's trouble,'" a friend told me, describing how she defuses arguments with her husband before they start. We know very well that certain actions, words, or situations are guaranteed to get a rise out of us. Sometimes all it takes to avert conflagration is a simple warning when you find yourselves playing too near the fire. If the provocation is deliberate, a warning won't be heeded. That means there's a hidden reason for the ensuing argument, and it's your task to discover it. When your partner is innocently cruising toward disaster, however, a blunt intervention can break the cycle.

❧

Instead of being pulled into your usual action-reaction pattern,
seize the red flag being waved under your nose and hold it high.
Sound a warning and create space for the conflict to simmer down.

What Silence Says

"Foot-and-a-half-long words."
Horace, *Epistles*

W hile I'm writing this, my husband is in the kitchen washing the breakfast dishes. The radio and TV are off; the cat is sleeping among the windowsill plants. Companionable silence reigns.

There is something that bonds us in the quiet time we spend, not exactly apart, but not together, either. I think of us in these instances as gyrating slowly, side by side, weaving our humble webs and growing a little older together. There is a peacefulness to it; a sense of certainty. I see that we don't have to be doing things together in order to "be" together.

A marriage is built as much upon the quality of its silences as upon its conversations.

Sitting with Pain

"The descent to Hades is the same from every place."
Anaxagoras, from Diogenes Laertius, *Lives of Eminent Philosophers*

Is there anything worse than knowing that you have dealt your relationship an irreparable blow? Perhaps it was unpremeditated, delivered in a backhand slash when all your hurts, petty and otherwise, drew into one screaming point and you lashed at him. Now you can't take it back. You can usually tell when you've cut this deep because your spouse goes silent—you have thrust to the quick, past where his anger can protect him. You'll feel his sadness at discovering that he is disappointed in you.

We all want to be there for our spouse in bad times. It's difficult to stick around, however, when we realize that *we* are the bad time. Understand that your partner won't be able to forget what happened, even if he is able to forgive you. Sitting patiently with pain of your own making is the only thing you can offer him now, after your sincere apology. At least let him see that although you can inflict pain, you are strong and loving and generous enough to live with its consequences.

◦◦◦

Some hurts cannot be repaired,
but at least they need not be endured alone.

Speak Up

"For it is feeling and force of imagination that makes us eloquent."
Quintilian, *De Institutione Oratoria*

Relationship experts exhort us to ask for what we want from our partner—otherwise how can he know our desires? Many of us become pretty good at routine requests: "Would you please clear the table?" "Can you pick up cat food on your way home?" "Call me if you're going to be late." But why is it so hard to make out-and-out demands—to say "Stop that" or "Touch me here" or "For Valentine's Day, I want flowers and to be taken out for dinner"?

Because we so desperately want to be understood, it's tempting to make mind reading a criterion for true love. In fact, true love is characterized by your lover's ardent *desire* to know and understand you in every dimension. Just as sharing your body is a conscious act of choice, so giving him your mind and heart must be, too.

∽∾

The willingness to open up—rather than
wait to be opened—is a hallmark of true intimacy.
It is the kind of courage love demands.

Holidays

"Courtesy and self-possession . . . arise out of a deliberate shaping of all things and from never being swept away, whatever the emotion, into confusion or dullness."

William Butler Yeats, *Essays and Introductions, Poetry and the Tradition*

Holidays can challenge marriage. It is difficult sometimes to be your real self when the family assembles. The pressures to fall into old roles and to create a perfect holiday combine to force us to do and be what we are not. You may be dismayed at the behaviors that emerge in your husband in a family setting. He may be equally dumbfounded by yours.

Rather than struggle through, realize that you have a choice: You can work to maintain your real selves within the holiday chaos; or you can opt to get together with family at other, less charged, times. Where families fall into particularly toxic patterns, the latter may be the only option. Working to remain genuine amid confusion involves remaining in constant touch with the self. Be patient and applaud your progress, however incremental.

∞

Holidays are not times to expect breakthroughs with family. Learn first how to manage yourself. The simple fact that you are acting different will begin to force a change in the family pattern.

The Real You

*"From childhood's hour I have not been /
As others were—I have not seen / As others saw."*
Edgar Allan Poe, "Alone"

There's no way around it—you will play each other's parents in your marriage, and you will play your own as well. Our parents were our first models for everything. It's natural that, when groping for ideas, we seize on the old, hard-wired responses. You'll hear yourself say things you swore you'd never say. You'll sense your spouse casting you in the part of his parent, without his even being aware of it.

It's the moment when you feel most compelled to act a certain way that you must stop, question, and examine. Ask yourself: What is the origin of this response? Can I stick by it? Is it who I really want to be in my marriage?

If it's too late to try things another way, go back later and figure out what happened. How did you really want to handle things? Share your discoveries with your partner. Next time, perhaps both of you will be closer to the mark.

$\backsim$

*Becoming your true self in marriage takes time.
Be patient, but keep stretching your wings.*

You're a Team

*"There is no more lovely, friendly and charming relationship,
communion or company than a good marriage."*

Martin Luther, *Table Talk*

Call me and I'll come pick you up." "You wait for the plumber; I'll get the dry cleaning." "You buy the movie tickets, I'll bring the snacks." Notice how you smoothly juggle a dozen daily duties, two people working as one body, tossing ideas, tasks, logistics, opinions, and plans back and forth like so many tennis balls. Celebrate all the small ways in which you jibe together. It's in the little things that the hard-won teamwork of marriage shows up most clearly.

∾

*Notice how far you've come,
not just how far you have to go.*

What Makes You See Red

"When there is much desire to learn, there of necessity will be much arguing."
John Milton, *Aeropagitica*

Repeated arguments are clues to important lessons available for the learning. I call them *"seeing red* moments." Upsetting as they may be, they reveal that each of you has a deep emotional stake in the matter at hand. That stake may be rooted in very old beliefs or events that act on each of you, igniting like fire and powder between you. Why are you being driven crazy by whatever-it-is, when another person might be irked, baffled, or even amused, and the matter could easily be settled with a little discussion?

Both of you will have to struggle to a common ground. The real solutions will come when you can dig out the real reason behind all of the commotion.

Stubborn conflicts give you repeated opportunities to come to the table with insights instead of accusations.

Priorities

*"Ah! when will this long weary day have end, /
And lend me leave to come unto my love?"*
Edmund Spencer, *Epithalamion*

Chores help us feel orderly, organized, and in control. They make for a smoother life. But trade them off with loving attention and you risk an imbalance of priorities. There will always be more chores to do, and dust will conquer us in the end. You have only your time on earth to love and be loved. Not all people are lucky enough to have the luxury of being loved. So do enough chores to be able to find your hat in the morning and your bed at night. Then remember what you were really put on earth to do: give and take your share in the cycle of love.

❧

*An orderly life is beside the point.
Connection is the only real hedge against chaos.*

Tuning In

*"I see thee better—in the Dark— / I do not need a Light— /
The Love of Thee—a Prism be— / Excelling Violet—"*

Emily Dickinson, No. 611

I don't want to talk about it." Who can resist such an invitation to probe, press, and ponder? We probably should probe if our partner's reticence impedes the unfolding of our marriage. But when our spouse blocks our access to his bad day, disappointment, or other upsetting event, we must respect his wish for silence. He may later decide to share his pain, his anger, or his sense of helplessness. We must treat that revelation gently, because anyone exposing a wound needs the most attentive care. But we also must find ways to heal him when he's shutting us out. We can give him the safe place he needs by staying close, staying quiet.

*Your spouse's way of needing you may not
be the way you expected. Provide what he needs,
not what you need, in order to feel better.*

Back Off

"Great wisdom is generous; petty wisdom is contentious.
Great speech is impassioned, small speech is cantankerous."

Chuang-tzu, *On Leveling All Things*

Sometimes your point is better made when you don't drive it home. In the heat of the moment, you will want to persist, push, make the result go your way. This can backfire on you if your partner ends up hearing your insistent voice but not your words. You're more likely to hit upon real resolution if you hold out for comprehension rather than insist on submission. Tell him, "I'd rather talk than argue. Can we cool down and discuss this?" If you give him room to have his point of view, he may be able to open himself to yours, no longer cornered and compelled to defend his position.

❦

Respecting your partner's boundaries opens
the way for him to respect yours.

A Gift

"My true love hath my heart, and I have his."
Sir Philip Sidney, *The Arcadia*

Think of a person whom you respect highly. Now, place your partner above that person. The man who has chosen to spend his life with you deserves the highest respect you can give. We sometimes treat those closest to us the most carelessly, because we count on their commitment to keep them close to us. We need to see their love as the rare and fragile gift it really is. The fact that it's fragile doesn't mean that it isn't strong; it does mean that our partner has exposed to us the most delicate, tender part of himself. We must guard it well, for if we abuse our partner's love, we are wounding the greatest gift he can give, leaving him with nothing.

∾

*Your partner's love is a gift he need never
have given. Treat him accordingly.*

Pick Your Prizes

"Slight not what's near through aiming at what's far."
Euripides, *Rhesus*

Make a list of the things you want from your marriage. Then cross off half the entries. There are only so many things one can strive for. Decide on the items that are most important, and work on those. Build a marriage that satisfies you in several crucial ways, and hope for the best on the rest. It is better to come away with a few things finely honed than to end up with nothing in particular.

In marriage there is no perfection. Expect some aspects of your union to be better than others.

Remember to Play

"Let the world slide, let the world go; | A fig for care, and a fig for woe!"
John Heywood, "Be Merry Friends"

Which of you is better at relaxing? Follow that person's lead whenever possible. We all know how to play. It's simply a question of allowing ourselves to remember what we already know.

Think about the things you do best and most happily together. Develop your daydreams until they're so real they won't be denied, compelling you to turn wishes into deeds. Enlist your partner's help in recalling shared good times. Remember how those times bonded you, wove your common history. The tapestry won't weave itself.

Take on your common dreams as projects. Weave them together. View your pleasures as being essential to your lasting partnership. Recommit yourselves to playing together.

❧

Play takes the lid off our joy. It unlocks
the self our partner loves most.

Rocky Roads

"Risk is what separates the good part of life from the tedium."
Jimmy Zero

No matter what you do, the road of your relationship will never be smooth. It is the nature of the road. There may be long stretches of easy riding; then suddenly you'll bounce through a succession of deep ruts. The same old fights spring up, plus some new ones. This is a good sign. It shows that your connection to each other is deepening: you are resisting one another on subtler levels. Beneath that resistance is a new terrain that you are protecting—entrance into yourself. This may be something you have never granted to anyone—yourself included. It's perfectly natural to resist your partner's attempts to gain access. But a living marriage is never static: It won't stand and wait. Work through the bad patches. There is good road on the other side.

Don't wait for the time when your relationship is free of conflict.
That is no sign of having arrived anywhere.

Free to Explore

"To give your sheep or cow a large, spacious meadow is the way to control him."
Shunryu Suzuki, *Zen Mind, Beginner's Mind*

et yourselves take separate paths in the common journey of marriage. It isn't necessary for you to know everything your partner is thinking and feeling. His mind is his own, as is yours, to be shared as an act of trust. Let an expansiveness enter your marriage, so that you are as free to be distant as you are to be close. It is not so much your closeness that binds you; rather, the freedom to be together, freely chosen. When you know this deeply and with conviction, then distance cannot exist between you.

Closeness is created not by knowing your partner well
but by allowing your partner to discover himself.

High Stakes

"With you I should love to live, with you be ready to die."
Horace, *Odes*

Old flames will flicker as long as the mind can consider what might have been. But you have not chosen the old flame, and neither has your partner. You chose each other. You chose because you wanted your lives to be made of something more than what hits us, willy-nilly, as we stumble through the space of our lives. When you chose marriage, you were ready for something more than transience. You sought transformation. A gift such as this naturally demands something in return: your daily presence—physical and emotional—in your marriage. Your marriage is only "there" to the extent that you are.

Don't wait for old flames to die. Instead, realize that both of you are playing in a much bigger game, for stakes that involve your very lives. Respect what each of you has willingly risked.

Play marriage as though your life depended on it.

Exclusive

"I knew a woman, lovely in her bones, /
. . . Ah, when she moved, she moved more ways than one; . . ."
Theodore Roethke, "I Knew a Woman"

That woman over there was giving me the eye," my husband said as we left the restaurant. "I think she thought I was, you know, *looking* at her."

We both knew he wasn't.

It's thrilling to know your partner only has eyes for you; leans forward over his dinner plate to hear what you say; makes sure your hat is snugly on your head before you step out into the cold. Your husband's undivided attention is a thing to revel in. Let him pay you this compliment. You and your partner are all there is, this night. You are a pair unto yourselves, exclusive to each other.

~ ~ ~

You are each other's one and only.
You can be, forever.

Mask of Anger

*"The thought beneath so slight a film— / Is more distinctly seen— /
As laces just reveal the surge— / Or Mists—the Apennine"*

Emily Dickinson, No. 210

Sometimes pain makes us lash out. We try to toss it away from ourselves by shouting, slamming things around, yelling at someone, blaming someone.

When your spouse erupts in anger that seems out of proportion to the situation, look to see if he is in the grip of pain. Perhaps he feels something coming on that he is powerless to handle. The only thing he knows how to do is fight it tooth and nail. Rather than yell back, placate, or try to convince him there's no problem, let your words and actions send a message of compassion: "I know you're having a hard time. I want to understand. I'm here to help."

Respect the powerful grip pain can have.
Give your partner a safe place where he can wrestle with it.

Lost and Found

"I wonder by my troth, what thou, and I / Did, till we Lov'd?"
John Donne, *The Good Morrow*

I think sometimes about what would happen if my husband died, suddenly, catastrophically. What frightens me is how certain I am that I would fall apart, as though he were the trellis and I the vine. It's unnerving to feel this dependent this early in my marriage. I like to be effective, efficient, independent. I fight the scary merging-instincts that have gripped me so fast, so hard.

The news is: We are helpless against those feelings. We cannot hold ourselves separate from our partner and feel intimate at the same time. Our job is much bigger and harder than that. Each of us must remain who we are, while losing ourselves in another.

⁀⁀

In marriage, you are not you, and you are not not-you.
You are a new entity altogether: a dynamic creation, becoming
what you will be while remaining what you were.

Free to Be

"Most people live . . . in a very restricted circle of their potential being."
William James, *The Letters of William James*

I'm catching a cold," my husband announced on the morning we were to embark on a trip. Wait a minute, I thought, I'm the one who gets sick on trips. He's not allowed to!

It's upsetting when our spouse shows a characteristic that we thought was reserved for us alone. We get peeved; we want him to stop his foolishness. *He's* not allowed to stomp around the house in fury; *he's* not allowed to fail miserably; *he's* not allowed to be captivating at a party—only we are. When did we start competing with him for attention?

Are you allowing each other to be all that you are?
Are you letting every dimension show?

What Moves in Silence

"Give me silence and I will outdare the night."
Kahlil Gibran, *Sand and Foam*

I think I've got his m.o. figured out," my friend said. She was describing her husband's *modus operandi*, a term used by police to describe a criminal's maneuverings. Sometimes we must be like detectives in marriage, ferreting out the motives behind our partner's behaviors. Much attention is paid to communication in relationships, but much more passes silently between partners: private discoveries quietly made, analyzed, and put to use in the marriage. If the conclusions we have drawn are not accurate, communication can help to correct our course. But it's in the tiny accommodations, the unspoken learnings, the uncontested acceptances we make that we demonstrate our passionate interest, our desire to understand, our commitment to making the marriage work.

❧

The bravest revelations and sacrifices in marriage
may be those that are the least discussed.

Oasis

"With thee, in the Desert— / With thee in the thirst— /
With thee in the Tamarind wood— / Leopard breathes—at last!"
Emily Dickinson, No. 209

Visiting with family can turn into an endless round of Main Events. It's easy to get caught up in the number of people to see and things to do, forgetting that you need time to return to yourselves for renewal and replenishment. Be sure to schedule some time for just the two of you to do a special activity. Perhaps it's a quiet breakfast at a sleepy café, a dodge into a dark movie theater, or an early-morning walk and chat over the newspaper. Reconnect with yourselves as individuals and with each other as a couple.

~ ∞ ~

When confusing surroundings threaten to pull you away
from each other, take time to remember who you are.

Remember This

"The beginning is the most important part of the work."
Plato, *The Republic*

Life can be too busy to allow time for making memories. You are forging many firsts in these years together; firsts that may become family rituals. Keep a camera handy, keep a journal of your travels, or make scrapbooks of special mementos from times of special joy. You think you will remember these times, but you won't, not in all their colors. Later these memories of your early years will become treasured family keepsakes.

These are important times. Make time for remembrances.
Consciously create a rich tapestry of shared history.

No More Squeaky-Clean

"'Oh, Jerry, don't ask for the moon. We have the stars.'"
Bette Davis in *Now Voyager,* screenplay by Casey Robinson

We work hard at making marriage free of negative emotions. It's a losing battle. The key is not in eradicating bad feelings but in deciding which ones are preferable to others. For myself, I'd rather be angry than bored. Anger dissipates, but boredom is a forever state. Perhaps you would gladly trade daily rage for a bit of the treadmill; for you, it could feel comfortably secure. There are no right or wrong choices here; only *your* choices. Take the pressure off: Instead of working so hard to eradicate every flaw, pick those you can live with, and narrow the field dramatically.

∽

Stop pushing for perfection. Instead,
choose your blemishes and count your blessings.

In Good Faith

"Let us be very strange and well-bred: Let us be as strange as if we had been married a great while; and as well-bred as if we were not married at all."

William Congreve, *The Way of the World*

Practice goodwill toward each other. That means being good-hearted, well intentioned, nonmalicious—even when it's a strain. Give each other the benefit of the doubt, assuming the best of each other. Goodwill and good acts are built through continuing trust. Good-heartedness can be difficult to maintain in stressful times, when the shorthand of sharpness seems expedient. But an innocent, playful spirit invites the desire to do right by one another.

Believe the best of your partner rather than demanding it of him.

Take a Break

"To do two things at once is to do neither."
Publilius Syrus, Maxim 7

id you think you could have all your "single" activities and be married, too? Wrong. It's a myth that you could have it all, if only you could figure out how. Besides, no one else is doing it nearly as well as they appear to be. Marriage takes effort. It fills your mind and your time. Some things are going to have to go by the wayside. You may later pick some activities up again while letting go of others. But don't exhaust yourself with wanting everything. In partaking of many, you give little to all.

Marriage takes, and takes hard.
Make room for the energy it demands.

Coming Together

"My morning incense, and my evening meal— / The sweets of Hasty Pudding."
Joel Barlow, "The Hasty Pudding"

My husband makes the pancake batter, using half the eggs called for by the recipe, the way he knows I like them. I set butter to soften atop the warm coffeemaker so he can have melted butter on his cakes, the way I know he likes them. We've developed our own unique recipe for spaghetti sauce that combines our separate tastes—thick and garlicky for him; bursting with mushrooms and onions for me. We shop separately and bring home treats for each other: the salt-free pretzels he likes; the corn chips I devour with salsa too hot for his taste.

We forge these traditions together, partly without realizing it; partly with the conscious wish to please each other. It's these little selfless acts and idiosyncrasies that make our union unique.

*Celebrate the small ways in
which you've created something very big,
something that embraces you both.*

Keeping It All Together

"Practice and thought might gradually forge many an art."
Virgil, *Georgics*

Are you getting what you need from your husband, most of the time? Are you supplying to yourself those things for which you're responsible: your sense of your own goodness, your faith in the goodness of the world around you? Are you providing what your partner requires, without losing yourself in him? These are the tasks of marriage: the simultaneous drawing of boundaries and bridges between you. You are not there to complete each other, yet you are a power together that you did not possess alone. You are not there to become each other, yet you experience a sensation of being one. Holding these opposing truths in balance takes enormous strength and energy. Expect wild seesawings sometimes.

Balance is not a static state. It is an accumulation of thousands of adjustments, a continual correction of course.

Old Business

"We reason deeply when we forcibly feel."

Mary Wollstonecraft, *Letters Written During a Short Residence
in Sweden, Norway, and Denmark*

I f you are careful, dredging up old, bad business can be constructive. It works best when you're able to bring up past hurts without needing to argue or press a point, but rather in the spirit of discovering the real emotional landscape of that time, free of the distortions that occur in the heat of the moment and cleansed by your desire to clarify and learn. Ask your partner to recall an incident: "Remember when . . . ?" Explain the feelings behind your response: "I got angry at you because I was hurt." Ask your partner how he experienced it: "What did you think/feel about . . . ?" Provide these healthy openings where past hurts can rise up, be heard, and be healed.

                    ⟲

*Carry the weight of your past between you
rather than letting it weigh you down.*

Solo

"No human being can really understand another,
and no one can arrange another's happiness."

Graham Greene, *The Heart of the Matter*

Marriage can be a lonely place. Some days you will feel misunderstood, unappreciated, unseen by the person to whom you want to be most visible. There is no more desolate feeling than to know that the "other" who has pledged to be beside you does not know or care about you in this moment. Only the remembrance of good times keeps you going. That, and the natural grit you are made of.

There are things about us our partner will never know, much less understand. We are all ultimately alone with ourselves. That is what makes the drive to relate to others so intense: It is saturated with the ecstasy of finding someone in whom we see something of ourselves and with the pain of realizing that not even this person will ever really know us.

❧

Loneliness is part of the human condition.
Marriage does not banish it.

Interference

"You are blind and I am deaf and dumb, so let us touch hands and understand."
Kahlil Gibran, *Sand and Foam*

Sometimes my husband and I must make our points five or six times before we understand each other. We accuse each other of not listening, but in fact it's a simple problem of assuming that "he is me" and vice versa. After untold hours spent seeking commonalities and honing our shadows to fit together, we are in the habit of seeing ourselves reflected in our partner. When we're forced to notice our essential differences instead, we feel disoriented and lost. We blame the other for not "getting" us, when in fact what is taking place is a perfectly natural process of self-differentiation.

You don't need to be on the same wavelength to succeed in marriage.
You just need to be able to ride each other's waves.

Your Partner's Wisdom

"Minds are like parachutes. They only function when they are open."

Sir James Dewar

His wife's really jealous," my husband said about a friend's spouse. "I told him, 'You've got to handle that right away. You can't just let it go. It's a basic issue that's not going to disappear.'"

Don't underestimate your partner's ability to see clearly through the mask of marriage. If he weren't a smart guy, you'd never have given him the time of day, much less have married him. How he arrives at his insights may be a mystery to you, but something's always cooking in his consciousness, be sure of that. Quiet your mind-chatter. Watch and wait for your partner's wisdom.

∽

The more preposterous you think your partner's
ideas are, the more of his unique sense they contain.
They reveal to you the mystery you married.

The View from Here

*"It takes so little talent to see clearly what lies under one's nose,
a good deal of it to know in which direction to point that organ."*
W. H. Auden, *The Dyer's Hand*, Part 1, "Writing"

Most of us are too busy living our marriages to notice how we act within them. To jar yourself loose from your habits, make an experiment of reacting differently than you normally do each time a problem arises between you and your husband. If what you usually do is get angry, try quiet acceptance or rational voicing of your views. If you normally adapt or accept, try waiting for the emotions to well up and make themselves known. There's no law that dictates the best way to act; the idea is to find the insights that are available to you when you step off the playing field and watch how you and your partner play.

∽

*Get outside yourself. Watch what you're
doing from a distance. The lessons from the bench are
as rich as those from the heart of the scrimmage.*

Which Fights Are Worth It

"'You alarm me!'" said the King. "'I feel faint—Give me a ham sandwich!'"
Lewis Carroll, *Through the Looking Glass*

We have more war if we try to cook than if we just order out," my friend said. This couple had decided that the expense of ordering out for dinner most nights was less costly than the battles that would ensue if each tried, at the end of grueling workdays, to foist the task of cooking onto the other.

It's wise to figure out which wars are worth waging. Fights take a lot out of you, leaving you with less to give each other in their aftermath. That doesn't mean one of you must cave in and do it the other guy's way. It does mean that you mutually agree on what isn't worth fighting about, *and* you agree on a solution that does an end run around the argument. Save your energy for the fights you really need to have: the ones that move you forward as a couple, not that reduce you to tantrums and tears.

❧

Don't waste your ammunition shooting at scarecrows.

Accept Doubts

"It was, of course, a grand and impressive thing to do,
to mistrust the obvious, and to pin one's faith in things which could not be seen!"

Galen, *On the Natural Faculties*

There is a part of me that holds back in my marriage, a part that says, "What would happen if all of this disappeared tomorrow?" This is the part of me that doesn't believe our best efforts will prevail; that wants to keep the lines of demarcation ("That's yours and this is mine") sharply drawn.

I don't know whether to fight this instinct or to heed it. Is this a voice of fear that should be overcome? Or is it a voice of reason, shunning the merge-everything attitude toward marriage still held by our culture and so dangerous for women?

I can only grope through this by asking in each instance: "Do I feel unsafe, in any way, by doing this?" If the answer is yes, then I must heed that warning or risk being less than honest with myself and my husband.

❧

For your own sake and for the sake
of your full presence in your marriage, listen
to all the conversations within, no matter how disturbing.

Getting and Spending

"A feast is made for laughter, and wine maketh merry: but money answereth all things."
Ecclesiastes 7:16

Money may be handled different ways at different times in your marriage. Much depends on who is earning more of it, whether there are imbalances in how (and by whom) it is being spent, and the amount of trust and power you accord each other in financial matters. As trust and power levels shift, and as the economic balance between you changes, expect questions of money to arise. Assume there will be discussions, even battles. Some subjects may be so hot that they are dealt with only indirectly, by anger or resentment leaking into other areas of your life together. This is a balance that may need frequent fine-tuning.

❦

In our culture, money symbolizes everything
from power to comfort. Expect its issues to appear in
your marriage, in many different guises.

Why Go to the Mat?

"The quarrel is a very pretty quarrel as it stands;
we should only spoil it by trying to explain it."
Richard Brinsley Sheridan, *The Rivals*

Not every spat has to be resolved. Sometimes we fight over silly things because we're tired, hungry, unwilling to be bigger than the problem, or just unable to expend the energy needed to avoid collision. Afterward we know it was a pointless game that would have been better risen above than thrashed out. You'll find that you and your husband will triage your arguments naturally: You'll walk away, cool down, and then reapproach and reengage as if nothing had happened.

⌒⌒

The decision to ignore a problem doesn't
always mean that you're letting things slide. Maybe
you're developing a sense of priorities.

Your Basic Fights

"'I am not an angel,' I asserted; '. . . you must neither expect
nor exact anything celestial of me—for you will not get it, any more
than I shall get it of you: which I do not at all anticipate.'"

Charlotte Brontë, *Jane Eyre*

Oh, yeah, we have our dog/housework argument once a week," my friend said, chuckling. That's about as often as my husband and I have our newspaper/clutter argument. Don't expect things to change just because you've had all the requisite arguments, reconciliations, and re-negotiations of who does what or who will stop doing what. Half the insanity of marriage is each person's persistence in doing what they want despite the other's energetic efforts to get them to do otherwise. You will make room for each other the way prizefighters move inches aside to pass in the narrow hallway outside the ring. There's no graciousness to it; only a supercilious tolerance. We're no different: only waiting to be left to our own devices so we can revert to our old ways.

❦

After marriage only a few things really change in our
habits and behaviors. Go for the important ones, and expect to keep
battling over the rest. It's OK. You can fight a lot without it
meaning anything, good or bad, about your marriage.

Play, Pleasure, Frolic, and Fun

"If you have two loaves of bread, sell one and buy a hyacinth."
Persian saying

Free time is called that for a reason. What you do during free time should make you feel free. What untethers you may not be what untethers your husband. It is not your obligation to clip your wings for his sake. Nor is it your obligation to make chores your main hobby. No one was ever barred from heaven for having ring around the collar. Heaven rewards integrity, and you can't have integrity without being integrated in all your parts: not just in how you relate to others, but also in how to relate to yourself; not just in how well you work, but also in how reverently you receive pleasure.

❦

Revere your free time and use it joyfully.
You cannot give when your cup is empty.

Fears

*"The opposite is beneficial; from things that differ
comes the fairest attunement; all things are born through strife."*
Heraclitus, *On the Universe*

My husband plays softball most summer weekends with a group of nice guys. I like to watch; sometimes I even take batting practice and shag balls. The guys like me; call me "sweetheart." Many are single and dub marriage "the old ball and chain." They don't see any inconsistency between that view and their affection for me. In their minds, the fearsome fantasy of "marriage" and the pleasant reality of "sweetheart" sit agreeably side by side.

I wonder if a man's fear of marriage is a fear of his desire to be consumed by love. If he casts the woman as the warden, temptress, or dominatrix, then it's all her fault if he loses himself to love. In contrast, women are taught to look forward all their lives to marriage. They struggle to hold themselves separate within marriage's unity, while a man struggles with letting himself go. Essentially we are working at cross-purposes, each person's fears fueling the other's.

❧

*We enter marriage from opposite sides, but with equal trepidation.
Respecting that we are both afraid can dissolve
much of the distance between us.*

The Unknown

*"The whole difference between construction and creation is exactly this:
that a thing constructed can only be loved after it is constructed;
but a thing created is loved before it exists.'"*

Gilbert Keith Chesterton, in *The Pickwick Papers,* by Charles Dickens

Y**ou** cannot be an open book to your partner. Telling your partner everything about yourself would exhaust both of you. Nor can you be a repository for all his anxieties, rages, and ugly secrets.

Each of us has a responsibility to carry our own frailties. We honor our partner by confiding our burdens selectively, not dumping them. We are not children anymore, believing that we can lose our fears and sins in an all-loving, all-giving parent.

The challenge of marriage is to approach it with all the hope of the child, having nothing of the child's innocence. This means holding our responsibilities on our own shoulders, being accountable for our own life, uniting ourselves with our partner, not by deluging each other with our pasts, but by shaping our future together with conscious, careful hands.

*True partnership is measured not by how well you know
each other but by how well you create together.*

Keep Learning

"Draw from others the lesson that may profit yourself."
Terence, *Heauton Timoroumenos*

Talk about other people's marriages, not as a point of gossip or self-comparison, but as a point of departure in discovering where the two of you stand on a given issue. Doing this gives you the chance to discuss your marriage in the abstract, without the emotional tension of a specific conflict clouding the conversation. Notice a couple's positives ("I like how they play off of each other, building on each other's ideas"), not just the negatives ("Do you notice how quiet and sad Fred seems around Sally? I wonder what's going on there"). Let others teach you about yourselves.

❦

Watch marriage at work in others.
Learn those lessons together.

Fits and Starts

"Improvement makes straight roads;
but the crooked roads without improvement are roads of genius."
William Blake, *The Marriage of Heaven and Hell*, "Proverbs of Hell"

W
hen we seek improvement in our marriage, we probably know better than to expect it to be immediate. What we may not know is that, once it happens, it isn't permanent. Change is like the universe: randomness is its organizing principle. As suddenly as new behavior arrives, just as suddenly it takes its departure. As with any skill newly learned, proficiency fades in and out as we struggle with the details.

❧

Have patience with the transient appearance
of improvements. Much is being moved forward on
many fronts. Understand that both of you are
doing the best you can right now.

Dirty Work

"True words are not beautiful."
Lao-tzu, *The Way of Lao-tzu*

Is someone in your household getting stuck being the bad cop? It's no fun to be the taskmaster, the wet blanket, and the heavy all rolled into one. Each of you must share the weight of broaching problems. That way no one gets cast as the mean parent, when all they're doing is the dirty work for two. If you're shirking, stop it. If you're doing all the work, refuse to take it on. Share the messiness.

In marriage there's no such thing as a free ride.

Compromise

D on't compromise if you're going to be mad about it. Folks will tell you that marriage is about compromise, but I think it has more to do with defining what you're *not* willing to compromise on, knowing that if you do compromise, you will take your dissatisfaction out on your spouse, one way or another. Understanding the subtleties of your own inner wiring is where marital maturity resides. Anyone can give up and give in. Not everyone can listen to the clamor within and come up with a sane, considered response that answers your needs as well as the demands of the situation.

∽

*The work of marriage is not in compromise.
It's in careful judgment, day by day, of where you
end and your partner begins. Work gently with
yourself in finding your way on this path.*

Rage

"The air is cleared; and in that clearer air, what do we see?"
Virginia Woolf, *Three Guineas*

Most of us have a standard way of handling anger that veers in one of two directions: We scream or we sulk. Permutations of each extreme include slamming doors or drawers, crying loudly, crying softly, burying ourselves (conspicuously) in a book, nagging, making sullen remarks, or sniping at our partner.

Anger is essential in the spectrum of human feeling. It is a form of feedback about what we need and want from life. Still, it's useful to find some new ways to handle it rather than be stuck with the one we perfected in the cradle.

Experiment with doing the opposite of what you're accustomed to doing when you're angry. If you usually yell, cry, or make scenes, try sitting quietly for a while by yourself. See if you can get at the hurts and fears that fuel your outbursts. Then perhaps you can confront your partner with useful insights rather than blast him with a verbal inferno. If you are a "silent treatment" expert, see what happens if you vent a little. Why is it so hard to take a stand on your own behalf?

❧

*In the thick of a conflict, resist the urge to react according to pattern.
Figure out what you need to do to keep the dialogue going.*

Stalemates Happen

"I prefer an accommodating vice to an obstinate virtue."
Molière, *Amphitryon*

In marriage, partners expend extraordinary amounts of energy trying to change each other. Our ability to challenge one another can lead to tremendous growth. But each of us has no-entry zones that must be respected, or there'll be trouble. Healthy change is the kind where everyone ultimately feels happier. Unhealthy change happens when someone's boundaries get violated. It's up to each of us to guard our own, and to respect our partner's.

Sometimes you will square off in a stalemate.
Not every problem is destined to be solved.

Slip-ups

"We live, not as we wish to, but as we can."
Menander, *Lady of Andros*

We begin marriage with the best of intentions. The busyness of life tends to rout out our good intentions, however, and suddenly we realize how long it's been since we did, said, or thought the ideals we started with. Then it's up to us to remind ourselves of how far we've drifted from our original purpose.

Ponder an area where your behavior has lost the starch of its original integrity. Keep your observations simple and free of censure: "I notice how critical I am of my partner. I will work on reframing the way I say negative things." Then, as you go about your days, be conscious of that one goal. When you hear yourself sliding into old habits, gently correct your course.

∽

Immediate perfection is not the goal. You are learning to apply the caring vigilance that sustains a conscious way of life.

Beyond Being Heard

"The way of a fool is right in his own eyes."
Proverbs 12:15

We spend a lot of time in marriage trying to make ourselves understood. We explain, demonstrate, explain again. Frequently what gets us into arguments is our anger at not feeling understood. The discussion can often degenerate into each side stubbornly trying to hammer home its message—unless you make a conscious effort to stand for something larger than the point you desperately want to make.

Beyond being heard and being right, what is the "partnership benefit" of the contention between you?

Let It Pass

"Love truth, but pardon error."
Voltaire, *Le Mondain*

When your partner makes a silly mistake, let it pass. What is gained by rubbing anyone's nose in their deficiencies? Wounds to the ego such as this seem minor, but they accrue over time and mar the atmosphere between you. For minor transgressions innocently committed and soon regretted, you will heal the breach sooner with understanding than with recriminations.

❦

Practice forgiveness in your marriage.
Both of you will need its favors.

The Fire Between You

"Love is a spirit all compact of fire, / Not gross to sink, but light, and will aspire."
William Shakespeare, *Venus and Adonis*

Your passion for each other is the source of sexual ecstasy, deep rage, and rapt hope. The fire between you fuels all energy, good and bad. Trying to extinguish negative energy between you will dampen other fires, too. Resignation, when reached in place of resolution, removes all hope from marriage. To be conflict-free should not be your goal. Perhaps your goal should be to tend the fire better, not to throw sand on the flames.

❦

*The problem may lie not in the marriage itself
but in the quality of the care it receives.*

Surprises

"Variety is the soul of pleasure."
Aphra Behn, *The Rover*

We meet like lovers on the sly: my husband riding back from softball practice on his bike; me sitting on a certain park bench where he will be sure to discover me. There's a shock of recognition; a smile of pleasure; a warmth in his eyes that says he knows it's a setup and he approves.

It's all part of finding ways to make our relationship new, introducing an element of the unknown when everything has become known. We tacitly agree to surprise each other in carefully orchestrated ways: to look the other way while one of us packs a birthday picnic, disappears down a bookstore aisle and reappears with a package tucked under one arm, or tosses out a gift catalog and asks which items rank as favorites.

As your marriage ripens, it becomes necessary to agree on such little tricks. The fact that both of you know what's up is half the fun: It shows that each of you is committed to keeping the romance alive. Certainly that's worth the price of a little spontaneity.

∽

Plan surprises. Give each other room
to create newness between you.

Odyssey to Joy

*"Come live with me, and be my love; / And we will all the pleasures prove /
That valleys, groves, hills, and field, / Woods or steepy mountain yields."*

Christopher Marlowe, "The Passionate Shepherd to His Love"

W e're climbing down a cliff at Nevada Falls in Yosemite Valley. Beside us roars a solid white sheet of water. The descent is nearly without trail, nearly vertical. We slide from rock to rock, sunburned and thirsty, shivering in the drafts thrown off by the freezing water.

"I'm scared," I whine. "I'm tired. I can't!"

"Come *on!*" my husband yells, sliding ahead. "We're almost at the Mist Trail. I'm not gonna let you miss the Mist Trail."

Without his cajoling, bullying persistence, I never would have made a memory to last my lifetime: standing triumphant and sopping wet in the shadow of the falls, looking up into a wall of water and seeing three perfect rainbows in the mist.

Marriage is often about persisting in the face of our partner's resistance. We are vow-bound never to stop trying.

❦

Sometimes we kick and scream all the way to exaltation.

Letting Go

"It is easier to fight for one's principles than to live up to them."
Alfred Adler

Which conflicts with your partner are you willing to let go of? It's not that you must get rid of them all; just that by now you are probably all too aware of those areas where your partner and you do not—and may never—agree. These may be as trivial as how you hang up your towels or as deeply infuriating as chronic lateness, nasty temper, or other offensive behaviors. The question is, Do you really want to fight about it for the next forty years? You will, unless one of you decides to drop it. Is it really worth the angst of battle?

Temporarily retire a few of your hot spots and see if your aggravation escalates or whether it is mitigated by a new peace at home—maybe even a willingness on your spouse's part to bury a hatchet or two of his own. Try it. You can always drag them out again if you really miss them!

 ༄

*Choose your battles, and bear in mind that
not every battle has to be won—or fought at all.*

Safety

"Let us run into a safe harbor."
Alcaeus, *Fragment 120*

When my husband comes to bed (usually hours after I'm asleep), he says I make "happy sounds." That's because he always touches my cheek or pats my shoulder or rubs my hair to tell me he's there. In response, half-awake, I make these little animal noises of contentment.

All of us have these small, helpless sounds. Maybe they come from the time of infancy, when noises were our only way to tell a parent what we liked and what riled us. Don't deprive your partner of these little noises. They tell him that he makes you feel secure and happy; that you will let him in this far; that you will let him comfort you. There's nothing of sex in it; it's more like a balm or a blanket enclosing you. Relish it. Honor him with it.

❦

It is not selfish or weak to be a helpless taker sometimes.
It lets your partner know how deeply you need what only he can provide.

Danger Signs

"Have a care therefore when there is more sail than ballast."
William Penn, *Some Fruits of Solitude*

Give each other clues that you're nearing the breaking point. Instead of surrendering to your usual reactive patterns, learn to sense when you're about to respond negatively, and alert your partner. He may have no idea he's pushing you to your limits. Or, if he is stuck in his own patterns, breaking the cycle may avert the chain reaction that leads to explosions between you. Try telling him, "I'm getting really angry" or "I'm feeling like I just want to run away. Can we talk about this later?" or "What you're saying is hurting me. We need to talk differently to each other."

Don't wait for the same old explosions to happen.
If you see trouble down the road, send up a flare.

Who's Got the Problem?

*"Now 'tis the spring, and weeds are shallow-rooted; /
Suffer them now and they'll o'ergrow the garden."*

William Shakespeare, *King Henry VI, Part I*

When we're doing the things in our marriage that feel unhealthy to us, it's easy to deflect anger away from ourselves and toward our spouse, making everything his fault. If you're doing the laundry for the umpteenth time and furious at him for not sharing the task, stop and ask yourself, Did he ask or expect me to do it? It sometimes happens that we are the ones expecting these things from ourselves. In your life together, which complaints are yours to own?

*Identify some behaviors that don't work for you anymore.
Clear them out, like old crabgrass.*

Being Heard

"When you fall into a man's conversation, the first thing you should consider is, whether he has a greater inclination to hear you, or that you should hear him."

Sir Richard Steele, *The Spectator*

W hen "do it *my* way" issues arise in marriage, we're rarely arguing over procedure. What we're often saying is, "*See* me. *Understand* me." When you find yourselves in an escalating cycle of stubbornness, break the pattern. Instead of making your point more strenuously, let your partner know that you understand what he's getting at; you realize that he has thought this out carefully; you know he has good reasons for having his opinions. Then quietly state your point of view. Once he feels heard and understood, your partner might be more able to hear and understand you.

∽

Compromise comes more easily when
both of you feel that you are being heard.

Positive Complaints

"The final cause, then, produces motion through being loved."
Aristotle, *Metaphysics*

My husband is a night owl, surfing the airwaves for late-night talk shows and bad horror movies. Invariably I'm asleep long before he puts in his appearance in the bedroom. For a long time I nagged him to come to bed earlier, citing all sorts of reasons, ranging from healthfulness to savings on the electric bill. Not long ago it occurred to me that it wasn't much fun for him to be badgered like this. Besides, I wasn't telling him the truth. It wasn't that I found fault with his night-owl ways (as my comments implied). I just missed him and wanted him next to me. That was a much more positive way to frame my requests. So now I say, "Hey, come to bed. I miss you." It doesn't always work, but that's beside the point. What I want is love and attention, which I promptly receive. And there's no more nagging at bedtime.

*Does your partner know the positive
reasons behind your complaints?*

Change

"Our doubts are traitors, / And make us lose the good we oft might win, / By fearing to attempt."

William Shakespeare, *Measure for Measure*

Does one (or both) of you hate change? If both of you hate it, the marriage can become paralyzed, unable to move from the status quo. If one of you hates it, the other always feels like a bizarre combination of cheerleader/browbeater/strategic planner: reassuring, cajoling, arranging, and generally standing on his or her head to make sure everything comes out right.

Change engenders anxiety in nearly everyone. You won't get anywhere with an anxious spouse until you address his root fears. Rather than trying to convince him that the plan is OK, locate what's causing his anxiety. Once that has been identified and understood, it may be easier to move forward.

Rather than arguing facts, try addressing fears.

A Promise

"*I cannot say / that I have gone to hell / for your love /
but often / found myself there / in your pursuit.*"
William Carlos Williams, "Asphodel, That Greeny Flower"

Now and then a conflict in marriage challenges us to the very end of our endurance. We feel we just can't take it another minute. We must escape this useless arena; find cool, free air. Where does the strength come from to resist, to stay, to take a breath and press on; to dig deep and find in ourselves one more minute, and the next, and the next?

Sometimes only a thin, strong thread ties us to our original commitment to each other. We stay only because we said we would. It is the power of our word that keeps us there, not because we want to be, need to be, or know what to do. We stay because we promised. That is a very scary place—a place bare of toeholds, stripped of ornament. That is a lonely place, for our partner is not there with us. He is hanging, alone, from his own cliff.

*There are moments of misery in marriage when
you will wonder how to endure. Remember that while
you are wondering, you are enduring. Trust your power to
cling to the rock when all the ropes have been cut.*

Solace

"A small rock holds back a great wave."
Homer, *The Odyssey*

Watch a toddler climb into his mother's lap for comfort and be assailed by the wish to be held, to disappear behind someone's protective arms. We all need this holding time when we can feel safe, for a few moments, from our worries. Provide plenty of this to each other. It's no weak thing to seek comfort. Only the strongest among us can admit we are weak.

∿

Give and take comfort often. Make it enveloping, physical.
Help each other shut out the world.

Ways of Giving

"I strove / To love you in the old high way of love."
William Butler Yeats, "Adam's Curse"

Your partner's contribution to your marriage will not be the same as yours. It will be all his own, formed by his interests, skills, and the unique construction of his commitment to you. It's easier to value your own contributions to the relationship—the sacrifice and selflessness of these are easy for you to see. It's much harder to view your partner's contributions in light of what they mean to him, rather than through the lens of your own values. Remember, he has a vested interest in making this marriage work. He, too, is trying.

❧

Notice the differences in how you and your husband work at your marriage. Try focusing on what he gives rather than on what you want.

Getting to Truth

We all have different ways of arriving at our truths. Some of us need to talk them out, refining our views word by word. Some of us move in silence, forming our ideas in thought, in an inchoate process that produces flashes of insights and in which the pieces of ideas fly together as if in chemical reaction.

How does each of you figure out what's true for you? Perhaps you want to talk; to boil an idea or problem down to its essence. Perhaps he finds talking an irritant, an intrusion on the silence he needs in which to sit and think. Let your partner do his process his way. Your unique contributions can complement, not oppose, each other.

❧

How you get there doesn't matter.
The fact that both of you get there is the crux of everything.

Exits and Entrances

"For God sake hold your tongue, and let me love."
John Donne, "The Canonization"

Everyone needs reentry time. Even when making as simple a transition as the daily arrival home from work, give each other space to unwind, regroup, rethink yourselves into the next sequence of action. Create a homecoming ritual that both of you enjoy. Maybe you always take a moment to kiss—really kiss—hello. Perhaps you share a glass of wine and talk about the day. Perhaps you cuddle together on the bed for a few minutes, just holding each other. Figure out what each of you needs to do in order to enter the evening as a whole, fully present person. Then provide this to each other.

No one can do the day without a break.
Give this to each other as an act of kindness.

No Perfect Fits

Life is filled with asymmetries—consider rocks, trees, the patterns of waves. Organic matter achieves a paradoxical kind of constancy in this. Since we are organic matter, we should expect asymmetries between ourselves and should never look for perfect union. A perfect thing couldn't survive the changeability of its environment.

Perhaps the incongruences between you are like the asymmetries that make nature so resilient in the face of disaster. Perhaps, rather than trying to file down your rough edges so you make a perfect fit, it is better to examine how the differences between you push you to new learnings, new strivings, new understandings never achieved on your own.

Perhaps it's your incompatibilities
that help you to survive.

Vacations for Two

"Perfect freedom is not found without some rules."
Shunryu Suzuki, *Zen Mind, Beginner's Mind*

A friend of mine loves to shop but isn't keen on outdoor pursuits. Her husband loves the outdoors but hates to shop. If they're not careful, vacations can be a tangle of wills. It helps, she says, if they give each other an escape hatch: At the outset of an activity, they clearly establish a way for the less enthused party to come up for air. That way no one feels that they're giving up too much, too often. That way they can join in with a will and stop when they've had enough.

$\backsim\!\!\sim$

Participation and enjoyment can be enhanced
by setting some simple limits.

Family

*"Nobody who has not been in the interior of a family
can say what the difficulties of any individual of that family may be."*

Jane Austen, *Emma*

Don't do each other's dirty work with family. If you or your partner have issues to work out with relatives, each of you must do it alone, on your own terms and in your own words. Asking your partner to act as go-between is an abuse of his caring for you. It's also just plain cowardly. Anytime you are tempted to do this, take it as a sign that there's much to be learned if you can face down your reluctance and carry through. Conversely, realize that it is healthier for your partner to do the hard work of growth on his own. Since no one can really know what we truly think or feel, we can't let others do the work that we must do ourselves.

⚭

*Take care of your own family business.
Expect your partner to do the same.*

What Price Compromise?

"Keep thy heart with all diligence; for out of it are the issues of life."
Proverbs 4:23

Too much compromise is not a good thing. It means you give up too much and feel too angry about it. It means you cannot wholeheartedly support your spouse, because your support comes at too heavy a cost to you. Excessive compromise resembles partnership but actually undermines it.

If you feel yourself pulling away from your partner, it's possible that on some level you are sacrificing too much to the marriage. This bears confronting, painful as it may be, because it will not go away of its own accord.

❧

Angry compromise is not the same as loving sacrifice.
Not all territory should be up for surrender.

Strangers

"*The human heart has hidden treasures, / In secret kept, in silence sealed.*"
Charlotte Brontë, "Evening Solace"

After much busyness that keeps you apart and preoccupied, are you startled to find yourselves with open time together? Without the daily minutiae of duties, news, and gossip, are you casting about for conversation? This can be unsettling, so much so that it's tempting to avoid instances that bring you simply together, with nothing to do. Don't shy away. It's natural to feel at a loss at first. It doesn't mean you are growing apart or any other significant thing. It just means that you need time to shift gears, to enter a quieter, more subtle level with each other. Give yourselves time to adjust to a slower tempo.

∾

Sit quietly with your unease with each other.
The process of reacquaintance takes its own time.

His Anger

> *"'How stern you look now! Your eyebrows have become as thick as my finger, and your forehead resembles, what, in some very astonishing poetry, I once saw styled "a blue-piled thunderloft." That will be your married look, sir, I suppose?'"*
>
> Charlotte Brontë, *Jane Eyre*

What is it about men that makes us feel safe when we're with them but also can frighten us to death? On the street, a sleek Jaguar screeches to a stop halfway into the crosswalk. My husband thumps on its hood, giving the driver some lip. Curses, rude gestures, and threats spill from the dark depths of the car. My husband itches to have the last word; I pull him away. I count on my husband's protective instincts, but I also see, when he uses it to wallop another man's masculinity, that it places him in danger. Will I ever get used to this?

∽

Male anger can be very frightening.
Don't hesitate to set limits around its use.

Altruism

"What thou lovest well remains, / the rest is dross."
Ezra Pound, "Canto LXXXI"

Not long ago my husband presented me with a small box of watercolors. "So you can paint on our trip to New Mexico," he said. Later he noticed a newspaper ad for a sale at our local bookstore. Three times he asked me, "Is there any book I can get for you?" Yesterday he left on my nightstand a yoga book he had bought some years ago. "You said your back was tense. I thought this might help."

One miracle of marriage is that we discover in ourselves and in our partner a true desire to help the other person become their best self. I think it is the part of us that is most noble, even the most godly, because it is about creation—not in our own image, but in the ideal image our partner wishes for himself. It is love that draws this from us, pushing us to rise to the occasion of the life we have determined to live, and to help our partner to do the same. Treasure and nurture these impulses between you.

$\backsim\!\!\backsim$

Generosity is you, leaving yourself.
Ecstasy has the same impulse.

Boasting, Bragging, and Praising

"He who is estranged seeks pretexts to break out against all sound judgment."
Proverbs 18:1

How often do you brag about your partner, or he about you? I'm talking about the proud sharing of accomplishments or deeds or talents that lets others know the deep respect you hold for each other. Do you admire your spouse, not for how well he complements you or how much he adds to your life, but for the very differentness of his persona; the ways in which he is unique and complementary wholly unto himself?

Think about what makes your partner unusual, someone to be noticed and honored. If you find yourself reluctant to praise him publicly, there's often a private power struggle going on. Search it out.

∽

Be alert to the nagging reluctances that tug you away from each other. They mean more than you think.

Giving and Taking

"What is yours is mine, and all mine is yours."
Titus Maccius Plautus, *Mostellaria*

When was the last time you just sat and let your husband "do" for you? It's difficult for many of us to allow someone else to serve us, with our only task being to receive appreciatively. Yet we think nothing of going out of our way to care for our spouse. We do it with love. Shouldn't we expect the same behavior from him? And if he is willing to do these things, do we expunge that willingness by saying things like, "That's OK, honey; I'll take care of it" and "You don't need to do that"? Why is it so hard simply to take, enjoy, and take some more, feeling that this is how things ought to be?

⁓

Sometimes it is better to receive than to give.
Taking lets us rest and regroup. It lets our partner
express his love for us through his actions.

Getting Lazy

"'Now here, you see, it takes all the running you can do, to keep in the same place.'"
Lewis Carroll, *Through the Looking Glass*

It's easier to feel stale than to bring fresh air into your marriage. It's easier to nitpick about old behaviors than to watch for new things to praise. Negativity is the impoverished soul's way of finding certainty in uncertain times: You can always count on being able to find problems.

Much more challenging is to seek the positive with full knowledge of the negative. Much richer is the ability to find new ways to enjoy each other when you know all the familiar ways in which to fight each other. Summoning up the positive is up to you. It is your act of will in marriage.

❧

Embracing the positive with open eyes
is marriage's challenge to venturesome souls.

Working from Silence

"In silence hushed, his very soul / Listened intensely."
William Wordsworth, "The Excursion"

My husband thinks a lot about our relationship," a friend told me. Although he rarely talked about their marriage, she said, she suddenly would see changes in behavior that indicated that he was doing important work on the relationship. Some people do not find talk easeful and comforting. They may prefer to wrestle with a problem in silence, with only a shift in action as the final proof of the labor they have done. If your partner is like this, you may think he is sailing along in uncaring oblivion. Not so. Perhaps he is simply entrusting the problem to a different process.

Silence doesn't necessarily mean that nothing is happening.

Handling You

"'Well, what does she want then?' said the flounder.
'Ah, flounder,' said he, 'my wife wants to be Emperor.'"
Grimm's Fairy Tales, "The Fisherman and His Wife"

Sometimes we act dreadfully. Our spouse puts up with it. All of us have blind spots that keep us from governing ourselves when it might do us the most good. Our partner stands there, right in the path of our hurricane. That he stands there at all is a wonder. That he jumps into the gale and does his best with us is testimony to the bravery love spawns. Let your partner give you a reality check when you need it. It may be the last thing you want to hear, but it could be the only thing that gets through.

∽

Sometimes we need to be set straight.

Feel It All

To feel life's joys deeply is also to feel its jagged edges. If we are sentient people, we can't escape feeling frayed at times by the force of our feelings. Days or weeks may pass when nothing seems right between us and our partner, and all we can do is hang in there and wait it out. Any truly passionate relationship contains the full complement of emotions, from fury to sensitivity that surpasses all understanding. You have to be a little crazy in order to be able to take it all standing up. Don't worry when things look dark; it's only one part of the spectrum.

✧

*Expect bad patches. You can only
"lose it" if you've found it.*

Between the Lines

"All poetry is difficult to read, / The sense of it is, anyhow."
Robert Browning, *The Ring and the Book*

Poetry is the language of excision: As much is said in what's left out as in what is included. Your partner is like a poem—epigrammatic, filled with nuance and unknowns, going at things slantwise. Don't expect a linear clarity in your reading of him. The richness is in what is unsaid or half-known, even to him. You will read him for years and learn something different every time. That makes for interest over the long haul. It also means that you must forgive yourself for not "getting it" all right away.

*Like a great poem, your partner's truths are revealed
layer by layer, over the course of many readings.*

Know When to Stop

"To go beyond is as wrong as to fall short."
Confucius, *The Analects of Confucius*

Once you've made your point in a discussion and know you've been heard, stop making it. Everyone needs time to process information. If you overwhelm your partner with grievances, at best he'll shut down and be unable to listen; at worst he'll counterattack in order to throw you off his back. Either way, the chance for resolution is lost. Respect your partner's need to turn aside and consider what you've said. Later you will have a chance to refine and define the details.

Handling conflict is 10 percent content and 90 percent technique.
Work slowly toward solutions, one facet at a time.

Choose the Positive

"To him who is in fear, everything rustles."
Sophocles, *Acrisius*

When I look for trouble in my marriage, I can always find it. Familiarity can lull us into expecting certain negatives in our partner. If we seek them, they will be there—along with a batch of others we're all too primed to see. This is not to say that we must play the cockeyed optimist, blind to flaws. It does mean that focusing on the negative is our choice to make. And the more we look, the more we will see. Why not assume that the same could be true of our partner's positive traits, and focus on those instead?

∽

Resist the pull toward the negative.
Give the positive equal time.

Keep Going

"To dry one's eyes and laugh at a fall, / And baffled, get up and begin again."
Robert Browning, *Two in the Campagna*

Bafflement is a big part of marriage. Continuing despite confusion is the strength you must apply. Often you'll have no clear idea why you're arguing, worrying, or feeling sad. It only gets clearer with time. And time's enlightenment can happen only if you get up, baffled, and start the journey again. Don't stand there in your puddle, insisting on clarity, before moving on. Sometimes the act of moving on is itself a step toward understanding.

Keep moving, despite confusion.
The learnings are in the going.

Staying Connected

*"Follow your love across the smokeless hill; /
Your lamp is out and all the cages still."*

W. H. Auden, "Madrigal"

I asked a friend to tell me the biggest lesson he had learned from his new marriage. "How to argue nicely," he responded. Arguing so as to stay in contact rather than retreat into sullen silence is a learned skill. Without contact there can be no resolution, so we must hone ways to get difficult feelings out into the open without sending each other into opposite corners of the ring. This is one sparring match where the only true victory happens when both combatants win.

∞

*Think of ways to stay in touch with your partner,
even when you're at odds.*

Share the Work

D o you have an emotional division of labor in your marriage? Does one of you take care of bringing up hot topics, while the other avoids until forced to look? Does one of you get angry, while the other feels hurt? These patterns take shape slowly but can become deeply entrenched over time. They have everything to do with your personalities, your pasts, and the unique balance of power in your relationship. This division of labor may be one way in which you complement each other. But getting stuck in its entrails is very limiting: the partner who always confronts feels like the "bad guy"; the partner who never confronts never learns this essential skill.

Discuss your emotional division of labor. Who is doing what? Then, just as you do with household chores, work at taking turns handling new duties.

$\backsim$

Stretch yourselves into new caretaking roles.
You will discover new respect for your partner's end of the deal.

You're on Your Own

"Talk sense to a fool and he calls you foolish."
Euripides, *The Bacchae*

No one understands the adjustments you have to make," a newlywed friend confided. People who haven't been married cannot comprehend the web of attraction, affection, and resentment that surrounds marriage. Indeed, sometimes even you don't understand why you're doing what you're doing in the moment that you're doing it. You are in an uncharted territory that millions have crossed before you, leaving no reliable trace of the road they followed for a safe journey. Your unique personalities will shape your paths; your invention will slowly order the chaotic energies each of you brings to your marriage. No one on the outside looking in can understand what an intricate dance this is.

❧

To outsiders, marriage is a cipher.
Ultimately no one can follow you on this journey.

Thinking Too Much

"'Tis safest in matrimony to begin with a little aversion.'"
Richard Brinsley Sheridan, *The Rivals*

Beware of endless analysis of your marriage. Constantly delving for the *why* behind every tiff or problem gets counterproductive when it's used as a way to avoid the risk of stating the way you feel, no holds barred. Don't sublimate your anger into endless discussion. It's OK to set your limits forcefully. You don't need to explain everything. When did feelings become things you had to make excuses for?

If you are one who always uses your head,
try losing your temper instead.

Accepting Help

It's late. I'm still at work. I call my husband, crying on the phone. "I can't get all of this done. I can't ever get it done. And what about dinner, and doing the laundry, and—" "Screw dinner," he interrupts. "I'll deal with the laundry. Do what you have to do, and come home when you're ready."

This is what I wanted him to say, prince that he is. So why do I reject his generosity, keep him on the line with protests that I don't mind cooking dinner and doing the laundry, really I don't? When our partner willingly takes over, why do we feel guilty? Have we failed in our task of taking care of everything? Have we sinned by putting ourselves first? Why is seeking pleasure, relief, or help loaded with such terrible ambivalence?

❦

Between true partners, there is no
need to keep tallies of debts owed. You will do
your share of his share in good time.

Be a Student

*"Learning is not attained by chance, it must be sought for
with ardor and attended to with diligence."*
Abigail Adams, Letter to John Quincy Adams

My husband is teaching me to shoot baskets. "Don't shove the ball at
the basket. Let it roll off your fingers," he says. Or, "Stay on the
balls of your feet. Otherwise I'll just step around you, like this."

There's much closeness to be had when one partner enters the other's
world as a willing beginner. It says we respect the other's reality, talents, and
the things that give them joy. It says we want to participate in their world, and
through that participation to come to know them better. What greater compliment can there be?

☙

*Take part in each other's interests.
Even the smallest sharing can sow closeness between you.*

Gales

"It is vain to look for a defense against lightning."

Publilius Syrus, Maxim 835

Seeking a smooth course in marriage may be our greatest vanity. Who is to say that a marriage without conflict is the pearl above all price? Once attained it might bore us, seem dead to us, because striving, moving, and pushing forward are the sensations that let us know we're alive and productive in the world.

Rather than try to avoid the lightning bolts of conflict, why not seek ways to turn the storm to your benefit? Soak up its lessons rather then try to forget it ever happened. Then you can be filled afterward with the quiet satiety that comes of making a conflict your own, running through it as it ran through you, turning your sails full into it and letting it push you and your partner into calmer, less contentious seas.

The best part of a storm happens when you emerge from below deck, green-faced, to hang onto the rail and swap stories of how you survived.

Solutions vs. Problems

"It is one thing to show a man that he is in error,
and another to put him in possession of the truth."
John Locke, *Essays Concerning Human Understanding*

Most arguments focus on problems, not solutions. When we do this, resolution takes longer because we must work past our partner's defense of his position; his interpretation of the problem, his criticism of how we have articulated the problem, and so on. Instead, try working backward: State the desired solution first; then let the problems percolate through this filter. Instead of saying, "Why do we always have to have the TV on in the evenings?" try, "In the evening, I like to relax and talk with you. Can we build in some time to do that, without the distraction of the TV?" Focusing on the wished-for result opens the way to problem solving, since your partner does not need to defend his position. Now you and he are working on the same side.

What do you need to do and say
in order to invite collaboration, not opposition?

'Til Death

"The ring, so worn as you behold, / So thin, so pale, is yet of gold."
George Crabbe, "His Mother's Wedding Ring"

D o I know?" the old man in the wheelchair quavers, staring at the trees through his sunglasses. "I don't know what I know, and I don't know what I *don't* know." The man's wife sits near him on a park bench, her hand covering his where it lies strapped to the arm of his wheelchair. "You know my friend Rose?" she asks. "Do I *know??*" he repeats. And the litany begins again.

I hope I will have the strength, should the time come, to show the tender patience this woman shows her husband, who barely recognizes her. It's hard to think that our decades together may end with one of us slowly slipping out of reach. The idea that we may have to watch each other die as part of our life partnership is barely conceivable. Watching elderly lovers care for each other shows so very clearly what it really means to commit for life.

☙

Marriage never ends. Not ever.

Choose Your Attitude

"We know the human brain is a device to keep the ears from grating on one another."
Peter De Vries, *Comfort Me with Apples*

"If both of us are cranky, someone has to un-crank," a woman told me. Do you work at sending out good energy in your marriage? It's not easy to make a conscious decision to reverse the thrust of a tense situation and create it as you want it to be rather than fall under its sway. It takes maturity, and an eye on the ball, to recognize that although it's tempting to keep swimming around in the old bad soup until our point is made, it is braver to select a different path to meet our ends. Choice opens new possibilities in marriage, invites us out of our rut.

*Attitude shapes action, and attitude is
a choice, freely made, every day.*

Losing Yourself vs. Letting Go

"Facts which at first seem improbable will, even on scant explanation,
drop the cloak which has hidden them and stand forth in naked and simple beauty."

Galileo Galilei, *Dialogues Concerning Two New Sciences*

It is essential to hold onto your own hopes, dreams, and desires in marriage. It's also instructive, sometimes, to throw your agenda to the wind, not in order to bow to your partner's wishes, but to see what possibilities open up when you remove the blinders that focus you on the tasks you've decided are important. Perhaps you'll discover new, unthought-of goals to pursue, having given yourself the space in which to see them. Perhaps you'll reach new understandings about your husband when you're able to observe his agenda as it operates independently from yours. Look for ways to move outside yourself and claim a wider sphere.

❧

Drop your focus from time to time to
see if having it still feels good.

Family Identity

"Love consists in this, that two solitudes protect and touch and greet each other."
Rainer Maria Rilke, *Letters to a Young Poet*

Your spouse knows you as a grownup. Your family, however, may treat you more like the child you were than the adult you have become. Your spouse can help remind your family that you are an adult, complete with opinions, ideas, skills, and dreams. In this way you and your partner can support each other when it comes to dealing with family—not by fronting for one another, but by treating one another like the adults you are. Seeing a spouse be respectful, deferential, and protective can be a powerful reminder to family members that yours has become a relationship of equals.

✺

*When you are with family, continue
to be yourselves with each other.*

Familiarity As Aphrodisiac

"The white chrysanthemum / Even when lifted to the eye / Remains immaculate."
Matsuo Bashō, *Conversations with Bashō*

A woman I know once observed that perhaps fear of abandonment fuels sex between partners prior to marriage. You really like the person, she explained, and you wonder whether or not they're going to stay with you. This uncertainty can provide powerful erotic tension. It is difficult to sustain that sense of tension as the months and years of marriage roll by. Rather than feel frightened by each other's unknowns, perhaps now it's time to revel in all you have discovered. It's time to contemplate the mystery of why you *haven't* abandoned each other, now that you can.

Now that love is here to stay,
how do you plan to keep it alive?

What's the Attraction?

*"I remember the neckcurls, limp and damp as tendrils /
And her quick look, a sidelong pickerel smile."*
Theodore Roethke, "Elegy for Jane"

What was it that attracted you to your husband, and him to you?
What later discoveries held your interest? Share these observations
with each other. We never tire of hearing all the good things our
partner sees in us—the ideal self that attracted him; the self we aspire to be. It
reminds us that we have potentials to live up to, and that our partner thinks
we can attain them. It reminds us to see the best in ourselves, especially on
those days when we feel least worthy of the best.

$\backsim \!\! \backsim$

*Tell each other often what you saw in each other, what you see now.
Being reminded why we are "The One" helps us to act that way.*

Sexual Spectrum

"Love's mysteries in souls do grow, / But yet the Body is his book."
John Donne, "The Extasy"

Sexual pleasure is the right of every woman. It's important to note that the focus and nature of our pleasure changes subtly and often. Sometimes sex is sharply satisfying. Sometimes it is more like a long, slow wave that crests, ebbs, and crests again. And sometimes our pleasure is in pleasing our partner. Both you and your husband will feel these changes in yourselves. Let them happen, and accept whatever is there. Sex need not feel the same, or be the same, all the time.

❧

Fully experience all your sexual
selves as they occur, together and separately.

Growing Room

> "*Dreams are necessary to life.*"
> Anaïs Nin, *The Diary of Anaïs Nin*

He walks to the very edge of the cliff, staring down into the canyon. She runs alone on city streets after dark. He applies to law school. She writes a book.

We must respect our partner's challenges and insist on the same respect for our own urges and dreams. No one moves forward in life without risk. If we dampen our partner's desire to risk, we cannot really have his best interests at heart. Making room for risk can be difficult, since the outcomes may affect us deeply. But the mutual strength you stand to gain is worth it, even when the risk is frightening and large.

We have a natural need to challenge ourselves.
There is no change in life without chance.

Hang In There

ESTRAGON: "I can't go on like this."
VLADIMIR: "That's what you think."
Samuel Beckett, *Waiting for Godot*

"Y ou aren't listening," my husband accuses. "You never listen!" It seems to me that all I do is listen, but my husband evidently is not getting that impression. Something has been lost in the translation. We are like two diplomats pounding the treaty table, yelling at each other in different languages, mystified by what appears to be the other's willful incomprehension.

When you are dealing with a problem that has deep roots for both of you, it may take a long time to understand each other's concerns. That's when cries of "You never listen!" tend to be heard. Take it as a sign that you may be getting somewhere, if only you can stick with it. Be patient and stay with the process. You will get there, one step at a time.

∽

When inspiration fails, persistence prevails.

Trial by Tempest

> "Give me a spirit that on this life's rough seas /
> Loves t'have his sails filled with a lusty wind, /
> Even till his sail-yards tremble, his masts crack, /
> And his rapt ship run on her side so low /
> That she drinks water, and her keel plows air."
>
> George Chapman, *The Conspiracy of Charles, Duke of Byron*

You never know if your boat will sink until you sail it on the open sea. Have you built her solidly, using the best seaworthy materials? Do you keep her lovingly, so what began strong remains so?

The strength of your marriage is tested by how it floats over time, on seas both rocky and smooth. Hitting rough weather quickly shows you where the weak spots are. Storms give you a chance to plug the holes. Storms aren't personal; they don't judge you as being good if you survive or bad if you don't. They are simply opportunities to sail your boat with courage and pride.

∽

If a storm comes, ride into it and let it really rock.
Storms show us that we can survive adversity
and find our way to calmer seas.

Basic Information

"Though marriage makes man and wife one flesh, it leaves 'em still two fools."
William Congreve, *The Double Dealer*

I hate getting up. I doze and delay, groan and grouse, until the last possible moment. When I try to catch those few extra minutes of delicious slumber, my husband warns, "You're going to be late for work! Come *on*, get up!" It doesn't make me move any faster. It just makes me grumpy.

Finally one day I had an epiphany: "He thinks that he's helping me. I've never explained to him that this is not how I need to be helped." The next time the cycle started, I gave him *acknowledgment* rather than anger ("Honey, I know you're trying to help me get up so I won't have to feel rushed and be late for work") and *information* ("But, you know, it would help me a lot more if you would just snuggle up with me for a few minutes and not mention getting up at all"). "Oh!" was his response. "Well, why didn't you say so?"

❦

Without information, our partner has
no way to make improvements.

Sex Talks

*"Full nakedness! All joys are due to thee, /
As souls unbodied, bodies unclothed must be, / To taste whole joys."*
John Donne, *Elegies*, "To His Mistress Going to Bed"

S ex is a very fine way of communicating," a friend confided. "When I'm not attracted to my husband, it means there's something to be discussed."

When something has blocked the flow of energy between you, the stress may first show up in the delicate channels of your sexual response. Rather than work at sex, it's more productive to work on the problem. The best route may be simple honesty and curiosity: "We haven't made love in weeks. I miss you. What's going on?" Patiently get to the bottom of whatever needs to be talked about. When the sexual channel opens, you'll know that healing has begun.

❦

*Don't let your problems sleep with you.
Your bed should be just big enough for two.*

Being Heard

"It takes two to speak the truth—one to speak, and another to hear."
Henry David Thoreau, *Civil Disobedience*

D o you or your husband often interrupt each other? Interruptions are really power plays to get the upper hand in a conversation. The interrupter is saying that he knows the answers better than you do. By allowing interruptions to happen, you're agreeing with him.

Everyone deserves to be heard. Being heard is how we make our presence known in our marriage. If your partner frequently interrupts you, let him know that you don't like his interruptions, that you see them for what they are. Stand up and be heard.

❧

*Express your truths clearly and without apology,
as many times as it takes to be heard.*

Staying Connected

I watch an older couple in a restaurant. Their entire meal passes without one word between them. They stare at their plates, at other diners, into space—anywhere but at each other. Where did the intense involvement, the obsession, of courtship go? I wonder. Must it end in this bland soup of mutual avoidance?

I believe there is another way, where the passion of the beginning becomes a kind of psychic understanding—a knowledge free of words—that allows you to anticipate the other's need for bread, pepper, solitude, talk. It's a knowledge that lets you see, without looking, the image of the other. It has nothing to do with the exhaustion I see in this couple's faces; everything to do with a transmutation of the explosive energy that fuels every couple's beginning. That is the energy I want to keep forever.

※

Every day you can either lose or find each other.
Work your connection like a muscle.

Taking Different Roads

"You think funny."
Greeting card message

My husband and I solve problems very differently. I talk and talk, groping through the issues, turning over possible solutions like pages in a book. Then, finally, with all the options clamoring in my head, I listen to my gut and take action. My husband ponders. His solution, when it comes, seems cut from whole cloth: rational, orderly, without the frayed edges I find so useful.

Each of you needs to respect the other's problem-solving process, even though you may never understand it. Your different methods add new colors to the mutual mix. Let go of trying to get your partner to think just like you. That is only about making you feel more comfortable, not about solving the problem at hand.

⌒

Your different ways enrich you both. Let them be.

Accept Comfort

"Listen to the little bird's voice; he has filled the whole thicket with honeyed song."

Aristophanes, *Birds*

et yourself be comforted by your spouse. When we're upset it's easy to catastrophize; to say, "Yes, but . . . " when someone tries to help us find a way out of our feelings. When you respond to your husband this way, you isolate yourself from the one person who knows you well enough to help you; who loves you well enough to stay close beside you as you walk the hot coals of conflict. Let him hold you. Let him help you pass through darkness.

You deserve release from pain. Let your spouse help.

Questions of Dominance

"When elephants fight it is the grass that suffers."

Kikuyu proverb

I t is unpleasant to witness someone wielding power over his or her partner. Men can do it to women by sheer physical force: the loudness of their voice; the hectic energy of their anger; their muscularity and size. Women can do it to men via intellect and emotion, cornering men in a thicket of their own desires or rage.

Hurting is not the sole province of one sex. Each of us has the power to do harm. Part of having integrity in marriage involves the responsible use of that power.

∽

Understand and respect your power over your partner.
Use it for the marriage's positive ends, not your own.

Unknown Territory

"Do not peer too far."
Pindar, *Olympian Odes*

It's tempting to think that each of you must tell the other *everything*, must have nothing but the sheer curtain of honesty between you. But sometimes it is an invasion to probe too deeply, to demand what our partner is not ready to share. Since it's folly to expect to know all there is to know about him anyway, let go of strivings and suspicions. All you can do is take care of *your* actions; make sure you are doing all *you* can do. Revelations will happen as they may, but your business must be to handle your business within the marriage. Know where your power lies, and focus your energies there.

∽

In the absence of complete knowledge,
seek complete engagement.

A Thought's Power

"You know I know you know I know you know."
Thom Gunn, "Carnal Knowledge"

I don't ever want to lose sight of the fact that my husband is my lover," a woman told me. "As soon as I think of him as my dowdy old spouse, I'm sure that's what he'll think of me."

Our thoughts about our marriage don't just reflect who we are; they shape our partner, as well. The bond between you is so close, so much like a membrane; expect attitudes to travel between you no less than words. If you are dissatisfied, consider that you may not be the only one with those feelings. Feelings are contagious. They move between you, shaping you together and separately. Respect the power of attitudes to sculpt behavior, and handle them with care.

What you think is who you become.

Same Old Story?

"Things must expect to come in front of us / A many times—
I don't say just how many— / That varies with the things—before we see them."
Robert Frost, "Snow"

Have you heard all your partner's jokes and stories before? Instead of tuning out, consider what the story reveals about your partner.

Each of us creates a kind of mythology of our lives, constructing events and circumstances according to the meaning they hold for us. The stories we repeat the most often are those that we have invested with the most profound significance. What do your husband's stories tell you about his hopes and dreams; his ideas about how life ought to be?

∽

Listen to your partner with ears
attuned to something beyond words.

Remaining Who You Are

"As soon as you know yourself, you will know how to live."
Johann Wolfgang von Goethe, *Faust*

Do you find yourself taking on the shadow of your husband? Do you say things he would say; do things he would do? A certain degree of mirroring is to be expected. Who could spend so long a time with someone and not have some degree of mutual transmutation occur? Some of these behaviors may fit you nicely. If they feel right and bring good results in your world, you are fortunate to have them. If they feel alien to you, don't hesitate to let them go.

Marriage should not change you in ways you don't approve of.

Surprises

"Five miles meandering with a mazy motion."
Samuel Taylor Coleridge, "Kubla Kahn"

By chance we find ourselves with a Saturday free of chores, errands, and obligations. We spend the morning in the West Village, poking around in old-book stores, checking out the contents of our favorite collectible shops. We discover a tidy little coffee bar where neighborhood folks lounge on benches outside, drinking caffe latte and flipping through the newspaper. We linger two hours over cappuccino and scones, engrossed in the best conversation we've had in weeks.

Make room in your marriage for the pleasure of the unexpected. Plan time with no plans, where these small moments of impromptu magic can happen. Those are the moments when you forge the memories that unite and comfort you—shining prisms in your common memory.

~

Marriage is built on its details.

Just You Two

"If ever two were one, then surely we. / If ever man were loved by wife, then thee; /
If ever wife was happy in a man, / Compare with me ye women if you can."
Anne Bradstreet, "To My Dear and Loving Husband"

We travel on the train, returning from a weekend spent with other couples. It's been fun but busy, and we hold hands and doze as the train hurtles us back to familiar life one-on-one. We are glad to be alone again; glad to be "just us" again; happy in the silences we create together, in which we dream or just lie back, thinking of nothing much at all.

The next time you have been out socializing, take note of the moments when you rejoin each other, just the two of you. It is a gift to have friends and a thrill to be with them. But there is a quieter thrill, a serene awareness, that comes from the time when you return, exhilarated or exhausted from your travels, to the cocoon you two have made.

Feel the contrast between the world outside
and the one you inhabit as a couple. Return to
each other often for rest and renewal.

Celebrate Yourselves

"And we meet, with champagne and a chicken, at last."
Lady Mary Wortley Montagu, *The Lover*

Today is our two-year anniversary: a time to consider how far we've come and how far we're going. Strangely, we have to keep reminding ourselves to celebrate. Making a big deal about our anniversary feels as odd as if we had suddenly decided to lionize our arms or legs. Seeing our marriage as existing apart from us is a foreign exercise.

Not surprisingly, we come up dry of ideas for fancy commemorations. Finally we end up doing what we do so well together: hanging out. At a nearby Mexican restaurant, we feast on green chile enchiladas and share a beer—a habit we got into on a recent trip to the Southwest. We talk, laugh, walk home arm in arm, just like we always do. The evening is exactly what an anniversary should be: a perfect celebration of what we treasure.

You have a natural reverence for each other.
Let yourselves be guided by your own lights.

Index